PETE BRISCOE

Stop Marching ~~~~~~~~~~~~~~~~ing

**100-DAY
DEVOTIONAL**
on finding rest &
freedom in Christ

Stop Marching, Start Dancing
By Pete Briscoe
Edited by Todd Hillard
A Book from Pete Briscoe, *Telling the Truth*, and Dunham Books, LLC
ISBN: 978-1-94264-27-3

Neither Pete Briscoe nor *Telling the Truth* nor Dunham Books, LLC is engaged in giving any professional counseling, psychotherapeutic, legal, accounting, or investing services. If professional advice is needed, please seek out the proper professional. We disclaim any loss, either directly or indirectly, as a consequence of applying the information presented herein.

Unless otherwise indicated, Scripture is taken from the THE HOLY BIBLE, NEW INTERNATIONAL VERSION®, NIV® Copyright © 1973, 1978, 1984, 2011 by Biblica, Inc.™ Used by permission. All rights reserved worldwide.

Cover and interior design by: Hope Certalic

Introduction

Do you remember how awkward it was when you learned to ride a bike? You could feel your body wobble from one side to the other as you struggled to stay upright—fighting against the pull of gravity. And all the while, you were reciting in your head a list of things to do in order to stay on the bike: keep your eyes straight ahead, don't look down, sit up straight, don't forget to pedal—you've got to pedal if you're going to stay on the bike... DON'T STOP PEDALING!!

Do you ever feel that same kind of uneasiness in your faith? Maybe you've put your trust in Jesus, but now you're keeping a list of things to do in order to be a good Christian: read your Bible 30 minutes a day, sign up to serve, make sure you're giving from your finances, and pray—you're supposed to continually pray... DON'T STOP PRAYING!!

I know your striving is well intentioned—I used to strive too. But the truth is Jesus didn't come so that you would become enslaved to working your way to holiness by doing things you think will bring you nearer to God. That's not the Good News He brought to the world.

The early church in Galatia struggled with striving too. They understood and believed that Jesus died for them and forgave their sins—but then they took their eyes off Jesus and starting following laws and rules in order to be "acceptable" to God.

At the beginning of chapter 3, Paul doesn't mince his words...

> *You foolish Galatians! Who has bewitched you? Before your very eyes Jesus Christ was clearly portrayed as crucified. I would like to learn just one thing from you: Did you receive the Spirit by the works of the law, or by believing what you heard? Are you so foolish? After beginning by means of the Spirit, are you now trying to finish by means of the flesh?* (Galatians 3:1-3)

So why do we so easily take our eyes off Jesus and begin marching to a beat that tries to earn His approval? That's the question I answer with Scripture in this devotional book.

I'm inviting you to dance to a new beat where you'll learn to live the Christian life in His power and not your own. Jesus is going to be your dance instructor each day. All you need is a willingness to grab hold and keep your eyes on Him.

And those who were seen dancing were thought to be insane by those who could not hear the music. —Friedrich Nietzsche

I want to invite you to a dance. I know that's not normal. But dancing isn't normal either. I mean, why would someone leave the predictable security of life, enter into the unknown, and risk looking like a fool?

Why? Because you might be hearing the call of the music, that's why.

In the continual blasting of life's noise, if you listen carefully, **you might be hearing the melody and harmony of the Holy Spirit, calling you to something different.**

> *"Then young women will dance and be glad, young men and old as well. I will turn their mourning into gladness; I will give them comfort and joy instead of sorrow. I will satisfy the priests with abundance, and my people will be filled with my bounty," declares the LORD.* (Jeremiah 31:13-14)

Do you hear the words? *Dance and be glad… gladness… comfort… joy… abundance… bounty…*

Many of us started out dancing *with* Christ but ended up marching for Him and other people instead. In the world, competing ideas and voices drown out the music and turn the dance into a march—a regimented discipline of denial and obligation.

- I should know. I've experienced it.
- I should know. I've caused it.
- I should know because I've rediscovered the better way.

Yes, I want to invite you to dance, because God invites us all into a dance with Himself and with each other.

Jesus, Leader of the Dance, silence my heart right now. Give me the willingness and the ability to hear through the noise of the distractions that dominate my life. Let me hear the music of Your Spirit again, calling me into grace, peace, freedom, rest, and trust. This week show me how to dance again, Lord. Amen.

DAY 2

dance

I always tell my kids if you lay down, people will step over you. But if you keep scrambling, if you keep going, someone will always, always give you a hand. Always. But you gotta keep dancing, you gotta keep your feet moving.
—Morgan Freeman

When I came to Dallas to pastor, I was a diligent marcher and I was good at it. When we arrived, the church was already marching. You could call it a *family-oriented march*. The motto was, "This church is a safe place to raise your kids." I started to lead us in a different march, the *seeker-sensitive march*. Our motto was, "This church is a safe place to hear a dangerous message." Our mission through the '90s was to help the lost, the letdown, and the "looking" find Jesus. We made church very comfortable for them, and we grew exponentially… yet there was a feeling that we were "a mile wide and an inch deep"… and it was true.

So in the early 2000s, we started the *disciple-making march*. Our motto was, "Each one reach one and teach one." We started asking the question, "What does a disciple look like?" We met for five years trying to figure out what discipleship was. We came up with all these linear processes and curriculums and models. We had some that were cool and some that failed miserably. We had the *community* model, the *life-group* model, the *Sunday school* model. We even had *model* models—model, model, model, model, model. **We had our programs intact but had forgotten the simplicity and purity of walking humbly with Jesus.**

> *Will the LORD be pleased with thousands of rams, with ten thousand rivers of olive oil? Shall I offer my firstborn for my transgression, the fruit of my body for the sin of my soul?* **He has shown you, O mortal, what is good. And what does the LORD require of you? To act justly and to love mercy and to walk humbly with your God.** (Micah 6:7-8 emphasis mine)

Looking back, in my mind's eye I see a bunch of North Korean soldiers marching in lockstep, with their legs perfectly synchronized and all of them absolutely scared to death they're going to mess up. We had created an army of marchers controlled by model programs… when all He was asking was for us to walk and dance with Him.

Oh Lord, by the power of the truth of Your Word and the presence of Your Spirit in me, reveal where I have submitted to programs and models of activity rather than to Your grace. Thank You for forgiving me for exchanging a humble walk with You for a march. Amen.

In spite of the Depression, or maybe because of it, folks were hungry for a good time, and an evening of dancing seemed a good way to have it.
—Lawrence Welk

I marched our church right into 2007. Then we got caught in a crossfire of our own making, as our congregation faced its inner turmoil. Our church stopped growing numerically and spiritually as the body struggled to get along. There was a disagreement amongst the leaders on how the disciple-making march should be executed.

I was preaching scared in those days, worried about what certain people would think. As a result, my preaching lacked passion and power. I told Libby, my wife, three times during that season that I was resigning. But I didn't…

In retrospect, I'm absolutely convinced that God was right in the middle of that mess, and here's why: **He was using our pain to get us to stop marching and start dancing.**

> *Praise the LORD.*
> *Praise God in his sanctuary; praise him in his mighty heavens.*
> *Praise him for his acts of power; praise him for his surpassing greatness.*
> *Praise him with the sounding of the trumpet, praise him with the harp*
> *and lyre, praise him with timbrel and dancing…* (Psalm 150:1-4)

In order for our church to start dancing, our leaders needed to start dancing. In order for our leaders to start dancing, *I* needed to start dancing. And that was the problem: nobody was dancing because *I* was a marcher, and I was good at it.

God will make us dancers one way or another, and if He has to use pain, He's okay with that.

Whether it's enduring a bad marriage, getting cut from the team, getting rejected by your dream college, getting a call from your oncologist, or clicking on that website one more time, God is using pain to invite us into the dance.

Father, by faith I accept the pain in my life as Your invitation to enter into the dance for which I have been created. Show me how the rules and regulations I've allowed myself to be placed under have hurt me and those around me. Lead me in the better way. Amen.

Love is a perilous dance too, you see. And if we stop dancing, we'll die. Don't ever stop dancing. —Kate Avery Ellison

Marching has its purposes in the military and in bands, but in Christianity, it can kill you. It kills your joy, it kills your energy, and it kills your passion for Jesus. And sooner or later, it's bound to burn you out, blister your feet, and bore you to death with its monotony. Ready for an honorable discharge? Here's how:

Recognize your need and your brokenness. Cry out to Him in honesty from a heart that is tired and desperate for the real thing.

Reject your flesh, self-righteous methods, standards, systems, and devotion to programs, etc.

Realize your hopelessness. Stop trying. Stop working. Stop striving. You might need to quit the committees and ditch duties. Just stop and let Him know that *you know* all your efforts are hopeless.

Rest in His finished work. Not just His crucifixion on the cross, but His resurrection from the grave. The crucifixion made it possible for your sins to be removed. The resurrection made it possible for you to find new life, to be a new creation. All that work was done on your behalf. It is finished.

> *"Come to me, all you who are weary and burdened, and I will give you rest. Take my yoke upon you and learn from me, for I am gentle and humble in heart, and you will find rest for your souls. For my yoke is easy and my burden is light."* (Matthew 11:28-30)

Listen, it takes courage to break ranks with those who are marching for God. You have to be a real fool to enter into the dance with Jesus (see 1 Corinthians 4:10). It's going to feel awkward and maybe even scary. **But the joy is worth it, every misstep of the way.**

Okay, Lord, You win. I'm calling it quits. I surrender. I'm tired of performing, I'm tired of conforming. I'm broken, hopeless, and exhausted. I'm done with the march. I want to rest in You as You lead me in the dance of grace. Amen.

dance

If you dance with your heart, your body will follow. —Mia Michaels

Sometimes, I wonder if we have a full understanding of the insidious life-sucking nature of spiritual marching. In most cases, it looks so darn good on the outside, but oh, the death it causes inside.

Eugene Kennedy wrote, "The devil dwells in the urge to control rather than liberate the human soul… We stand by a dark forest through which fearful religious and political leaders would force us to pass in single file through their exclusive pathway of righteousness."

The unspoken lie of man-made religion is this: If you *do* right, then you will *be* right. **But because of what Jesus has done, we are all right; and now there's nothing left to do but dance in that truth with our eyes focused on Him** (rather than being so consumed with ourselves and our actions). It's time to be free. It's time to dance with your heart… then your body will follow.

> *Praise the LORD.*
>
> *Praise God in his sanctuary;*
> *praise him in his mighty heavens.*
> *Praise him for his acts of power;*
> *praise him for his surpassing greatness.*
> *Praise him with the sounding of the trumpet,*
> *praise him with the harp and lyre,*
> ***praise him with timbrel and dancing,***
> *praise him with the strings and pipe,*
> *praise him with the clash of cymbals,*
> *praise him with resounding cymbals.*
>
> *Let everything that has breath praise the LORD.*
>
> *Praise the LORD.* (Psalm 150, emphasis mine)

Come on. Quit marching! The dance is all about praising God for what He has done and truly experiencing the indwelling Christ moment by moment, day by day. Because Jesus, my friends, is the essence of the dance.

Lord of the Dance, show me specifically today where I am still marching for You, rather than celebrating life with You. Set me free! Set my heart free to praise You! Give me an intense awareness of Your presence around me and in me. With all of my heart, I will follow You as You lead me in this great dance. Amen.

Run, John, run, the law commands but gives me neither feet nor hands.
Tis better news the Gospel brings. It bids me fly, it gives me wings."
—John Bunyan

Learning to dance seems so unnatural at first. That evening I first stepped onto the honky-tonk dance floor in Fort Worth, I was so, so self-conscious. Why? Because I was concerned about how everyone viewed me. Why? Because I had always focused on my performance and effort and behavior and marching.

Learning to dance is scary stuff, and some never try—not in a honky-tonk and not with Christ. Why? Because I'm convinced that most of us are afraid to step into the freedom that Christ offers. Why? Because we've got this huge misunderstanding about how God views us, and that turns most of us into marching slaves.

If marching is slavery, dancing is freedom.

- Freedom to live
- Freedom to enjoy
- Freedom to obey
- Freedom to share
- Freedom to fail
- Freedom to start all over again
- Freedom to move with the music of the Spirit

> *It is for freedom that Christ has set us free. Stand firm, then, and do not*
> *let yourselves be burdened again by a yoke of slavery.* (Galatians 5:1)

If marching is all about my work for Him, then dancing is all about the finished work of Christ for you and for me. The believers in Galatia started out dancing—and then some false teachers came in and got everyone marching, performing, evaluating, and all wrapped up in themselves.

When I ask you to dance, I'm not inviting you to be a contestant on *Dancing with the Stars*. It is not you in the spotlight with everyone judging you and people texting their evaluations from all over the country.

I'm inviting you to step into His grace, to step into the truth of who you already are in Him. Why? Because our whole world is wired to judge you by your performance, and it is natural for us to feel like God works that way too. He doesn't. He's got a competely different system. It's called grace. And we can believe in it, rest in it, and then dance in it like no one is watching.

Oh Jesus, by the Truth of Your Word and the power of Your Spirit, live through me today.
I stand firm against the voices and powers that want to enslave my soul. I exchange fear
for freedom! Amen.

Notice: The beatings will continue until morale improves. —Motivational poster in an office breakroom

I've been marching almost my entire life… that is, until I learned how to dance.

Marching is slavery. It's adhering and imitating and fitting in and doing what you think you're supposed to do. It's a life of stress and strife. It's performing and observing traditions and following rules and trying to please and emulating and replicating… (Well, it's at least *attempting* to do all of that—but who can live up to it all?) The thing is, we didn't start off in Christ as slaves—neither did the Galatians.

> *You were running a good race. Who cut in on you to keep you from obeying the truth? That kind of persuasion does not come from the one who calls you.* (Galatians 5:7-8)

Who cut *me* off from the truth of grace? It was Mrs. Olson, my first grade teacher. I was a free kid before I met her. I was dancing like I was created to dance—and then she gave me my first elementary school report card. For the first time, I saw in black and white what it meant to be "satisfactory" (smiles and kudos) and "not satisfactory" (frowns and head wagging).

I'm telling you, life started to get screwed up with our elementary school report cards, the major induction into a world where we are judged for our effort, behavior, and performance. We get beat up under that system every day in school, at work, in marriage, and in ministry too. And the beatings don't just come from others. Back when I was marching, I was either beating myself up, disappointed in myself, comparing myself to others, or proud of myself, depending on how well I performed.

But what if—I'm just throwing out a hypothetical here, okay?—what if, way back in the day, your first grade teacher had loved you intensely *just the way you were*? What if she had sincerely and passionately enjoyed you *just because she adored you*? **And what if she had given you an A+ before you even started the class, confident that you would become exactly who she wanted you to be?**

Okay, so that wasn't just a hypothetical. You recognize where I'm going with this, don't you…

Master Teacher, it was for freedom that You loved me and set me free. Open my eyes so that I can see those who "cut in" on me and cut me off from the truth of grace. Open my mind to imagine the transforming implications of You loving me and already giving me an A+ in life. Amen.

dance

If you can't get rid of the skeleton in your closet, you'd best teach it to dance.
—George Bernard Shaw

Did you ever read something in a book or hear a promise in an infomercial and think, *Yeah, that could be true. Maybe it is. Oh, I HOPE it's true.* I feel that way about God's timeless promise of grace. It's like I know in my head that I'm loved by Him as I am, but because I'm so used to getting beat up with the performance legalism of the world, my heart is skeptical.

The truth, whether we feel like it or not, is this: In Christ, God has already given you an A+ in the class of life. Because of Christ's finished work, Christians already have an A. The threats of failure, judgment, and condemnation have been removed. We're "in" for forever. Nothing we do will make our grade better, and nothing we do will make our grade worse.

In His life, by His death, and with His resurrection, Christ, our substitute, secured for us the A that we come into this world longing for and yet, are incapable of securing for ourselves. We don't need to add anything to it. Paul put it this way:

> *For I am not ashamed of the gospel, because it is the power of God that brings salvation to everyone who believes: first to the Jew, then to the Gentile. For in the gospel the righteousness of God is revealed—a righteousness that is by faith from first to last, just as it is written: "The righteous will live by faith."* (Romans 1:16-17)

All the pardon, the approval, the purpose, the freedom, the rescue, the meaning, the righteousness, the cleansing, the significance, the worth, and the affection that we crave and need are *already* ours in Christ. That's not just our hope; that's God's promise of truth for life today.

Father, I thank You that the same operative power that made me a Christian is the same operative power that keeps me a Christian: Your unconditional, unqualified, underserved, unrestrained grace through the completed work of Christ. Show me, right now, the implications of this truth. Amen.

It's not whether you win or lose, but how you play the game. —A common phrase… spoken only to losers

The Bible isn't all good news. The book of Romans, for example, is brutally honest about our starting GPA in life. In chapters 1 through 3, Paul dishes out the evaluation: **We all start with an F.** It doesn't matter if you're a religious person, a totally hedonistic person, or a really judgmental person; every single person starts with an F because sin has separated us from God.

> *All have sinned and fall short of the glory of God…* (Romans 3:23)

But then, chapters 4 and 5 of Romans describe the stunning way we get an A. This is the cram sheet for the most important exam question in all eternity, and this is the stunning answer:

> *Therefore, since we have been justified through faith, we have peace with God through our Lord Jesus Christ, through whom we have gained access by faith into this grace in which we now stand. And we boast in the hope of the glory of God.* (Romans 5:1-2)

You get the A not by your works. It's by trusting in the finished work of Christ. We "make the grade" with God by totally different standards than the way the world judges us. And I'm telling you, this higher truth is one of the indispensable keys to unlocking a life of freedom.

Holy Spirit, I stand in Your grace, by faith, ready to face this day. I celebrate God's glory and the hope grace gives right now. Set me free to dance with Christ because of what He has done. Amen.

When I thought God was hard, I found it easy to sin, but when I found God so kind, so good, so overflowing with compassion, I smote upon my breast to think that I could ever have rebelled against One who loved me so, and sought my good. —Charles Spurgeon

I respect people who fear that dancing in a honky-tonk could lead to sin. Yeah, I sure wouldn't step foot on the dance floor with anyone but my wife. Some people also fear that if we quit marching for God and start this crazy dance with Christ, sin could be the result as well. I mean, if the teacher gives you an A, why not blow off the class?

- You would miss out on all the richness the teacher has in store for you.
- You would have to live with a mess of consequences.
- You would find yourself a slave to sin again anyway, marching for this tyrannical master.

All true—yet there is an even more fundamental, deep-down core reason: Dancing in Christ sets us free *not* to sin.

> *Grace and peace be yours in abundance through the knowledge of God and of Jesus our Lord. His divine power has given us everything we need for a godly life through our knowledge of him who called us by his own glory and goodness. Through these he has given us his very great and precious promises, so that through them you may participate in the divine nature, having escaped the corruption in the world caused by evil desires.* (2 Peter 1:2-4)

Get this! It's through the grace of God's power that we are "given everything we need for a godly life" today. You already have your A in the grade book because of what Christ did on the cross and through the resurrection. When you really come to grips with that fact, you would never for an instant consider blowing off His class.

Jesus, thank You for giving me Your divine power. Allow me to grasp the incredible truth that I "participate in the divine nature" because Your Spirit lives in me. I'm Your student, in class, ready to learn. Take me dancing this weekend. Amen.

DAY 11

dance

People have asked me why I chose to be a dancer. I did not choose. I was chosen to be a dancer, and with that, you live all your life. —Martha Graham

Back in the day, the church at Corinth was an absolute mess. Sure, they were a holy mess because they were saints in Christ, but their behavior was pathetic. Paul could have started his letter to them like this: "Hey, what's wrong with you people? You're a bunch of idol-loving, sex-crazed, unfaithful, egotistical, self-centered, greedy babies! Stop that! Get your act together!" But do you know what? Paul never starts his letters like that. He always starts by telling them who they are in Christ first.

> *Paul, called to be an apostle of Christ Jesus by the will of God, and our brother Sosthenes, to the church of God in Corinth, to those sanctified in Christ Jesus and called to be his holy people, together with all those everywhere who call on the name of our Lord Jesus Christ—their Lord and ours… I always thank my God for you because of his grace given you in Christ Jesus.* (1 Corinthians 1:1-2, 4)

This is the pattern throughout the New Testament, and it's a powerful pattern that sets us free to live as God created us to live. First we realize the truth about who we are in Christ, then comes the "expression" part. "Marching" focuses on the commands without even thinking about who we are in Christ. "Dancing" begins when we rest in what He has done and who we are because of it.

Listen, when someone realizes they really are an A+ student because of Christ, they will start to live like it. That's totally backwards from the way it works in the world… but then again, isn't almost everything Christ did?!

My Heavenly Father, I am a mess too, just like the Corinthians. I thank You from the bottom of my heart for the grace You have given me in Christ Jesus, that I've been set apart. I thank You that I am called to be holy, chosen by You to be Your child. Amen.

dance

You can't get second things by putting them first; you can get second things only by putting first things first. —C. S. Lewis

Who you *are* in Christ comes first. What you *do* comes second. It's absolutely essential that we get the sequence right. We can only *do* when we know who we *are*. C. S. Lewis taught that. Paul and the New Testament writers almost always outlined their messages that way too. Check out Paul's letter to the Ephesians. He nails the message by reminding them of who they once were, then he tells them who they are now, and finally, later in the letter he tells them how to live in light of their new Life.

> *As for you, you were dead in your transgressions and sins, in which you used to live when you followed the ways of this world and of the ruler of the kingdom of the air, the spirit who is now at work in those who are disobedient. All of us also lived among them at one time, gratifying the cravings of our flesh and following its desires and thoughts. Like the rest, we were by nature deserving of wrath. But because of his great love for us, God, who is rich in mercy, made us alive with Christ even when we were dead in transgressions—it is by grace you have been saved. And God raised us up with Christ and seated us with him in the heavenly realms in Christ Jesus.* (Ephesians 2:1-6)

Verses 1-3 make it clear that we all started with a big fat F in the school of life—with words like *disobedient, deserving of wrath* written in the comment section of our report card. BUT everything changes at verse 4. *"Because of his great love for us"* we are:

- Made alive with Christ
- Saved by grace
- Raised up with Christ
- Seated in the heavenly realms

Finally, in verses 8-10, Paul concludes the sequence with the words that emerge from us because of His work in us:

> *And this is not from yourselves, it is the gift of God—not by works, so that no one can boast. For we are God's handiwork, created in Christ Jesus to do good works, which God prepared in advance for us to do.*

C. S. Lewis had it right. Who you are in Christ comes first. What you *do* comes second. It's absolutely essential that we get the sequence right.

Oh Lord, don't let me ever brag about my A. I see now that I had nothing to do with it. I am Your workmanship, Your masterpiece, created in Christ Jesus as a new creature in Christ. Now, do with me as You wish today. Amen.

Somebody just gave me a shower radio. Thanks a lot. Do you really want music in the shower? I guess there's no better place to dance than a slick surface next to a glass door. —Jerry Seinfeld

Marching is pretty safe. Dancing can be dangerous. I mean, you could trip and fall. Others might point and criticize as you move in new freedoms. It really helps to know that, in Christ, we already have the A. But do we *really* know this? I mean, is it a deep-down truth in your soul? Paul prayed that it would be!

> *For this reason, since the day we heard about you, we have not stopped praying for you. We continually ask God to fill you with the knowledge of his will through all the wisdom and understanding that the Spirit gives, so that you may live a life worthy of the Lord and please him in every way: bearing fruit in every good work, growing in the knowledge of God.* (Colossians 1:9-10)

He clarifies what he prays we will know a couple verses later:

> *Once you were alienated from God and were enemies in your minds because of your evil behavior. But now he has reconciled you by Christ's physical body through death to present you holy in his sight, without blemish and free from accusation.* (Colossians 1:21-22)

Wow. Talk about a reversal! We once had a big fat F because we were alienated, enemies, and evil. But we tried our hardest and turned things around, right? Nope. We dance freely and safely because of what *He* did. Oh, the joy of resting in the finished work of Jesus and the ongoing work of His Spirit!

Oh Spirit, give me the knowledge of God's will, through Your wisdom and understanding, that I will really know that by Jesus' sacrifice I have an A—that I am holy, without blemish, and free from accusation today and always. Amen.

There is a time for everything, and a season for every activity under the heavens: a time to be born and a time to die, a time to plant and a time to uproot, a time to kill and a time to heal, a time to tear down and a time to build, a time to weep and a time to laugh, a time to mourn and a time to dance… —Ecclesiastes 3:1-4

When it comes to dancing, timing is everything. For example, most people believe that you actually have to dance "in time" to the music. (Although I proved this axiom to be categorically false.) Other people believe that the best time to dance is in the evening and on the weekends. That might all be true at a honky-tonk, but what about our spiritual dance with Christ? I say the best time to dance is *now*. Why? For no other reason than His love and mercy, God has chosen to give us that A+ in the class of life. It's a central theme throughout the whole New Testament, *so go for it! Dance now!* Through Christ we are in the 100th percentile, and will be *eternally*.

Consider these words penned by Peter:

> *Praise be to the God and Father of our Lord Jesus Christ! In his great mercy he has given us new birth into a living hope through the resurrection of Jesus Christ from the dead, and into an inheritance that can never perish, spoil or fade. This inheritance is kept in heaven for you, who through faith are shielded by God's power until the coming of the salvation that is ready to be revealed in the last time.* (1 Peter 1:3-5)

Translation? You can't lose your A, my friend. It's written in His book in ink, forever. You can rest in that. You can stop marching and start dancing now because of His never-ending grace.

Oh Jesus, nothing in the world works like this. By faith, show me the next steps You want me to take in the eternal dance of Your grace. Amen.

Live your truth. Express your love. Share your enthusiasm. Take action towards your dreams. Walk your talk. Dance and sing to your music. Embrace your blessings. Make today worth remembering. —Steve Maraboli

Okay, confession time: This whole idea about getting an A before you even take the class? I didn't make that up. I borrowed it from a book, a really solid book called *Jesus + Nothing = Everything* by a guy named Tullian Tchividjian. (How's that for a last name? Tullian needs to buy some vowels from Vanna, in my opinion.) Tullian didn't make it up either. He quotes Steve Brown whose daughter, Robin, found herself enrolled in a really difficult English literature course. Certain that she was going to fail and that everyone else was much smarter than she was, she and her father went to the teacher to beg for a transfer to an easier class. As soon as the door was closed, she began to cry. The teacher said, "Robin, I know how you feel. What if I promised you an A no matter what you did in this class?" Robin couldn't believe it, but agreed. The teacher opened up the class roster, wrote in Robin's name, put a big A as the final grade, and said, "Now, get to class."

I told my kids this story and they were like, "Dude. Where's that teacher at my school, right?" I mean, who wouldn't want to be in that class? Who wouldn't want to be taught by that teacher? I would!

How does knowing you have an A before the class even starts change your experience in that class?

- There's less pressure.
- There's less bragging.
- There's less competition.
- There's less self-flagellation.
- There's no fear of failure.
- There's more joy.
- There's more life.
- There's more focus.

Why? Because for people with transformed hearts, there's *freedom*.

> *It is for freedom that Christ has set us free. Stand firm, then, and do not let yourselves be burdened again by a yoke of slavery.* (Galatians 5:1)

Leader of the Great Dance, I'm tired of marching. I'm tired of comparing myself to others and feeling either inferior or superior. I'm tired of being afraid of failure. Some days, I just want to give up and disappear into the crowd. By Your unchanging, unfailing Word, convince me that I have an A in Your class of life, not because of anything I have done, but because of what You did. Now set me free to learn like I have never learned before as we dance through this life. Amen.

If you pour oil and vinegar into the same vessel, you would call them not friends but opponents. —Aeschylus

Some things were never designed to be mixed together… *ever*. I mean, think about it. Would you ever put motor oil in your coffee? I don't think so. Would you ever seat an Aggie next to a fan from the University of Texas? Not unless you wanted to see another Civil War.

Well how about marching and dancing? Can you march under legalism and dance to the music of the Holy Spirit at the same time? Think about it. **Dancing is all about the work of *Christ*; legalism is all about *our* works.** The Gospel is all about the finished work of Christ. Under the law, we work to earn His favor and/or the favor of men. Don't get me wrong: **The law of the Lord is good… but once the law has done its job, it's time to dance!**

> *But before faith came, we were kept in custody under the law, being shut up to the faith which was later to be revealed. Therefore the Law has become our tutor to lead us to Christ, so that we may be justified by faith. But now that faith has come, we are no longer under a tutor.*
> (Galatians 3:23-25 NASB)

My concern is this: the Church today perpetuates a hybrid mixture of law and grace, of marching and dancing; and this mixture subverts our dependency on and joy in Christ's work. It messes up everything, just like motor oil would pollute your coffee—and my guess is that this mixture is much more prevalent in the Church and in your life than you might think.

God of grace, search my heart. Show me Your ways. Open my eyes to the legalism in my own life, and the rules and regulations around me. Oh Lord, may they never be mixed in my heart. Amen.

dance

Legalism says God will love us if we change. The gospel says God will change us because He loves us. —Tullian Tchividjian

The book of Galatians is a searing letter of correction from Paul to the people who lived in the region of Galatia. It's interesting that when Paul wrote to the Corinthians (a city immersed in flagrant sins of the worst kind), he still found something nice to say about them. Not so the Galatians. The people in this region had fallen for something so severe that Paul used the most intense words possible to wake them up. What could possibly have been so serious?

The Galatians had started out dancing in grace, but then they started marching under a new form of legalism.

Theologians actually call this the "Galatian heresy." Essentially, after Paul left the region, a group of devout Jewish believers moved in and said, "Yeah, everything Paul says is true, *but* we need the law too." They were trying to mix law and grace, marching and dancing. So how does Paul start this critical letter to the faithful followers in Galatia? By bringing them back to the undiluted simplicity and power of the Gospel.

> *Grace and peace to you from God our Father and the Lord Jesus Christ, who gave himself for our sins to rescue us from the present evil age, according to the will of our God and Father, to whom be glory for ever and ever. Amen.* (Galatians 1:3-5)

This introduction to this critical letter is a potent reminder to us today to never, never mix the purity of the Gospel with anything else.

Jesus, my Lord and my Savior, Lord bring me back to the simplicity and purity of Your Gospel today. I praise You that You gave Yourself up for my sins and that You rescued me from the evil in this world, by grace. I rest in that now. Show me where I am trying to add anything to Your work by my own works. To You alone be the glory for ever and ever. Amen.

dance

The main thing between you and God is not so much your sins; it's your damnable good works. —John H. Gerstner

The tone of Paul's letter to the Galatians gives me shivers. I mean, it really sends a chill down my spine. And the irony of the situation makes it all the more powerful: **The Galatians were really trying to go the extra mile, trying to work their hardest, trying to keep all the rules and regulations… And Paul rips them up and down for it? Is that fair?**

> *I am astonished that you are so quickly deserting the one who called you to live in the grace of Christ and are turning to a different gospel—which is really no gospel at all. Evidently some people are throwing you into confusion and are trying to pervert the gospel of Christ. But even if we or an angel from heaven should preach a gospel other than the one we preached to you, let them be under God's curse!* (Galatians 1:6-8)

That seems harsh, but it's not. **By adding marching to dancing and legalism to their grace, the Galatians were actually "deserting the one who called you to live in the grace of Christ."** *Desertion. Going AWOL. Perversion. Abandoning their post.* Yes, it's *that* serious. Grace is *that* important. Adding anything to the Gospel of grace is as destructive as adding used motor oil to your coffee; it's really "no Gospel at all."

Oh Lord, open my eyes. Give me the wisdom to see the seriousness of compromising Your amazing grace. Show me that legalism is not devotion to God, it is deserting God. Please Lord, point out one area where I am marching away from You rather than dancing with You. Amen.

DAY 19

Legalism breeds a sense of entitlement that turns us into complainers.
—Tullian Tchividjian

Most cults are masterful when it comes to mixing law into grace. And they make it sound so good. They tell you they have the "complete gospel," that they have the "full gospel," that they have "progressive revelation." The bottom line is the same message:

"Jesus? Yes! But you also need to…" "Grace? Yes! But you also need to…" Yeah, that's the mantra of grace-destroying heresy. Adding requirements to the Gospel implies that grace is not crucial and Christ's work is not sufficient. Paul sounds the alarm:

> *If anybody is preaching to you a gospel other than what you accepted, let them be under God's curse!* (Galatians 1:9)

But adding requirements to grace and Jesus' work is rampant within the core of our church communities too, more so than we care to admit! **The theology of the misguided becomes our biography anytime we buy into the lie that we can march in a way that improves our position with God.** How might we do this?

- Listening to the right music
- Wearing the right clothes to church
- Adopting a certain political agenda
- Serving the poor
- Getting a theological education
- Praying
- Serving on committees
- Abstaining from alcohol or drugs
- Tithing
- And on, and on, and on…

Don't get me wrong. All things can be for good, but only if they are an extension of grace and the power of the Holy Spirit living through us. Otherwise, it's just legalistic works that pollute the power of the Gospel in your life by mixing two things that never belonged together: Law and grace.

Oh Jesus, by the power of Your spirit in me right now, show me the good things I am doing for the wrong reasons. Show me where I am still trying to earn favor with You by my works rather than dancing in the freedom of Your Spirit and letting Him work through me. Thank You. Amen.

dance

Truth will rise above falsehood as oil above water. —Miguel de Cervantes

Satan will do anything he can to distract us from Christ. *ANYTHING*. And once he has lost us to God's grace, he'll do anything he can to keep us from experiencing our freedom in Christ. One of his favorite tactics is the mixture of law and grace that creates a false gospel.

Listen, Satan is smart, and he knows you're not that stupid either. So he's not going to try to feed you straight motor oil. I mean, who would go for that? Right? But he's going to try to trick you by mixing that oil into your coffee… He's going to try to inject marching into your dance through lies that destroy the whole thing.

And one of his favorite tricks is getting us to try to *please* people rather than simply *loving* people.

> *As we have already said, so now I say again: If anybody is preaching to you a gospel other than what you accepted, let them be under God's curse! Am I now trying to win the approval of human beings, or of God? Or am I trying to please people? If I were still trying to please people, I would not be a servant of Christ. I want you to know, brothers and sisters, that the gospel I preached is not of human origin.* (Galatians 1:9-11)

Please be honest with yourself and think about this. You can keep all the rules from a bitter heart. You can keep all the rules and still have no desire for God's glory whatsoever, and it is very likely that you will be tempted by Satan to try to keep all the rules so people will notice you.

Worst of all, you can keep all the rules and never love God and never love people even once. That's why keeping the rules is such a dangerous thing, because you can actually do it and completely miss out on experiencing Life.

Jesus, I believe that You are absolutely all I need. I believe that life in You is an experience of the Holy Spirit transforming me and expressing Himself through me. I don't always live this way. It's so easy to start marching to someone else's agenda again and again. But today, I'm stepping out onto the dance floor again, listening to Your music, ready for You to lead me again. Thank You! Amen.

Former Iranian hostage Barry Rosen touched down on an American tarmac 30 years ago and spilled into the arms of a wife and two young children lost to him during 444 days of captivity. —Michael Hill

There's just something about seeing someone set free that lights me up. I mean, when a person has been held hostage for much too long, the whole body has a language it speaks when it realizes freedom has come.

As the absence of captors and walls sinks in, the one set free spills into the arms of those waiting. Tears of gratitude flow. Emotion comes as both laughter and sobs. As the moments of captivity fall behind and only freedom exists—both now and in the future—the truth comes that nothing can take this freedom away. It's been given; it's finally here. I love seeing those scenes in the news because they're a powerful reminder of what Jesus has done for our souls:

> *It is for freedom that Christ has set us free. Stand firm, then, and do not let yourselves be burdened again by a yoke of slavery.* (Galatians 5:1)

There is a certain joy that comes from freedom, and that joy is anything but silent. As the embrace of our loved ones loosens, the chatter begins. This joy fills our emotions to overflowing—we can't contain our praise. This joy writes the story upon our lips and we can't silence it—it becomes the music of our life.

And we must dance. Because we are free.

We join in the song and the dance of the Israelites who, after generations of slavery, erupted into celebration.

> *He brought out his people with rejoicing, his chosen ones with shouts of joy.* (Psalm 105:43)

We have nothing left to do with that freedom except proclaim it and live it, hoping that our story and our dance can show other captives the way out.

Lord, teach me how to live in this joy. I am free and Your Spirit in me is rising. My joy is a gift unwrapped in the presence of freedom—I cannot contain it! It stretches my body to the limits of praise. My arms in the air—unshackled and with praise—and my feet moving in step to the rhythm of freedom. Live through me, Lord, this unscripted life of freedom. Lead me in a dance of joy that never ends. Amen.

dance

Normally, he liked boundaries. Boundaries were the safety net. Boundaries kept people on the right path. But right now, he felt like rules were made to be broken… —Heather Burch

A dozen kids were playing street hockey. I could hear the coarse language flying faster than the puck, but didn't think it was bad enough to ask my kids to come indoors. Then, *Whap!* I heard the front door slam.

"The kids outside won't listen to me. I told them we don't say those words, but they said it's a free country and they don't have to follow my rules!"

"They're right," I told him. "Our rules are for *our* family."

"But I don't like it when they say that stuff."

"Yeah, me either. But do you like playing street hockey with them?" He nodded. "Then relationship trumps vocabulary," I told him.

Every group of people has "tribal rules" that those in the group are expected to abide by. My child knew our family's standards of behavior—*our* tribal rules. What my boy didn't realize is that he can't enforce our rules on people *outside* our tribe—that isolates everybody from everybody. **Our rules aren't intended to keep others out, but to keep our tribe aligned.**

The early church debated over tribal rules during their time of expansion. Persecution had intensified and early Christ-followers fled Jerusalem. They settled in new towns where Gentiles— outsiders—were being exposed to the Gospel. These outsiders didn't share the Jewish roots of the first believers, and cultural clashes arose concerning food laws and circumcision. Some thought Jewish tribal rules applied to all:

> *"Unless you are circumcised… you cannot be saved."* (Acts 15:1)

Think about it! This was a big deal. The core message of grace was at stake. I love the way Jesus' brother James chimed in:

> *"It is my judgment… that we should not make it difficult for the Gentiles who are turning to God."* (Acts 15:19)

And neither should we. Coming to faith in Jesus is hard enough for some people. Why would we make it more difficult for them by requiring our tribal rules about language, dress, music, food, etc.? Isn't it time that we drop the role of enforcer and become champions of grace outside our tribe?

Lord, as I dive into these tribal rules, show me which ones I expect others to live by. Show me which rules I've slung around the neck of a fellow human, a weight that keeps us from dancing together. Amen.

Those who dance are considered insane by those who can't hear the music.
—George Carlin

In the early '70s, my parents were leading a church in Wisconsin that served 300 hard-working, salt-of-the-earth Midwesterners. But there was a family whose older children didn't fit into the suit, tie, and Bible-carrying culture of Sunday mornings. So they started a Bible study at their house; and before they knew it, 200 hippies were gathering in their home. Soon enough, the hippies asked, "When do we get to come to your church?"

For one Sunday, attendance at our church nearly doubled. But it was a major culture clash as the tribal rules of our church had a head-on collision with those from the outside. The church "won." The next Sunday only 20 hippies came. The third Sunday, only one showed up—one courageous soul came barefoot in holey jeans and sat cross-legged on the floor right in front of the platform.

That young man stayed and attended membership class with those suit-clad members who gave him the cold shoulder. At the end of the class, as part of his membership requirements, he stood to share his story:

"I didn't know Jesus until two months ago. I've got so much to learn, and one of the things I've learned is that I'm *supposed* to hang out with you people… **I've read the Bible. I've got to love you, so I'm gonna choose to love you even though you have shown no love to me.**"

Ouch.

Then he asked, **"Can I talk with someone about how we can do this better?"** An older man stood up and invited the hippie to lunch. Together they came up with a plan to build relationships between the two cultures. Tribal rules faded. Divisions erased. Invitations extended. Isolation broken… and several pairs of bare feet graced the doors of our church once again.

All because someone chose to show love where no love had been. All because someone chose to leave behind the tribal rules so the tribe could grow and be free and love as they all learned to dance in grace together.

> *So in Christ Jesus you are all children of God through faith… clothed…*
> *with Christ. There is neither Jew nor Gentile, neither slave nor free, nor is*
> *there male and female, for you are all one…* (Galatians 3:26-28)

When we let the tribal rules fall, a diverse Kingdom reigns.

Father, the better choice is always You. I'm carefully wrapping my arms around Your waist, putting both my bare feet on top of Yours, and waiting for the dance to begin— let Your steps be mine. Amen.

Some people believe holding on and hanging in there are signs of great strength. However, there are times when it takes much more strength to know when to let go and then do it. —Ann Landers

Culture clashes are as inevitable as wrinkles, parking tickets, and rush-hour traffic. Tension resides in differences between people when something transitions from old to new. The same is true within the church where we desperately hold on to our tribal rules that have nothing to do with the Gospel—and there are times when it takes much more strength to let go of these rules rather than hang on.

Here's the deal: Since its infancy, the body of Christ has debated what it means to be a follower of Jesus. As Christianity poured out of Jerusalem, the words they used to describe the Gospel came from their tribal Jewish heritage: Jesus *became* the Passover Lamb. Jesus *fulfilled* the law. The heart should be *circumcised* and tender toward God.

But then the new non-Jewish audience embraced the Gospel. These Gentiles knew little of Jewish customs and terminology. Food laws were foreign, Jewish festivals irrelevant, circumcision not practiced, and the Sabbath was just another day.

Bam! A clash between old converts and new converts ensued. Many Jews insisted that Gentiles were not acceptable to God until they acted Jewish too.

But God had something new in mind. In a vision on a rooftop, the Lord showed Peter that **the way of acceptance was the way of unity.**

> *"Do not call anything impure that God has made clean."* (Acts 10:15)

Later, Peter witnessed the Spirit of God pour out on a room full of Gentiles, and he understood that **it is impossible to invite people in when we require adherence to rules that keep them out.**

> *"So then, even to Gentiles God has granted repentance that leads to life."* (Acts 11:18)

It's really simple.

- **One Gospel: God accepts all who are in Christ.**
- **One body: In Christ, there is neither Jew nor Gentile.**
- **One rule: In Christ, love others as God loves you.**

Lord, give me Your love and acceptance for those who don't adhere to my tribal rules. Guide me into relationships that are outside my norm. Teach me how to invite the outsiders in so that they, too, may know You cherish them. Amen.

The people heard it, and approved the doctrine, and immediately practiced the contrary. —Benjamin Franklin

Are tribal rules really so dangerous? After all, some boundaries are healthy and certain behaviors *are* inappropriate. Right? If I let go of the do's and don'ts in my faith, am I not compromising the Gospel?

Great question. Here's a great answer: **Tribal rules are not faith fundamentals.** For example, "Jesus is God" is not a tribal rule—it's a core belief. And when I say, "I am saved by grace through faith," this is not a rule. It's *the* foundation of the Gospel. That's not what we are talking about. **Tribal rules add to the fundamentals of faith. As a result, these rules undermine the simplicity of the Gospel.**

For example, a theological tribal rule might require baptism as a means of salvation. A cultural rule might say you have to dress a certain way. A social rule might say you shouldn't be friends with the "heathen." Such rules add to the Gospel of grace. When you add to grace, you erase grace; and isolation takes its place.

Think about Peter. He was living this new life of freedom and relationships. In the Jewish culture, to share a meal with someone is to share God's blessing with them, and Peter was eating with lots of non-Jews. But all of a sudden, he stopped and isolated himself from the Gentiles, essentially saying, "I take back the blessing of God."

Paul caught wind of Peter's vacillating, and he was not happy.

> *When [Peter] came to Antioch, I opposed him to his face, because he stood condemned.... He used to eat with the Gentiles. But... he began to draw back and separate himself... because he was afraid of those who belonged to the circumcision group.* (Galatians 2:11-12)

Reread that verse carefully. **Peter's ministry could have come to a stop right there and then because of his tribal rules and because he caved under the pressure of the legalists.** Those religious rules outside the Gospel are dangerous, causing serious separation between us and those God wants to love through us.

I'm saying we let those rules go and cling only to the core of the Gospel. God is a God of unity. There is no room for separation in the realm of reconciliation.

Is there someone out there God is calling you to eat with today?

O Lord, by the power of Your Spirit, show me where I let my religious rules and the expectations of others separate me from those You love. Show me where I can reach beyond my rules and invite others into the dance today. Amen.

dance

A man can no more diminish God's glory by refusing to worship Him than a lunatic can put out the sun by scribbling the word "darkness" on the walls of his cell. —C. S. Lewis

Since cultural clashes are nothing new under the sun, it's comforting to know they serve a purpose. **The early church is a great example of how hard times can lead to good things.**

Shortly after Jesus' ascension, a spark of persecution ignited within the walls of Jerusalem. Stephen's bold speeches caught the attention of a few established council members who were trying to keep everyone marching to the religious rules. The council charged Stephen with blasphemy—working against God. In response, Stephen charged them with apostasy—the rejection of God Himself.

Tempers flared and the council sentenced Stephen to death. As the rocks hailed down upon Stephen, they were sure they would extinguish the fire of grace in the crowds. The council members had no idea that the Lord would use Stephen's death to fan the flames of freedom instead. Like embers from a single fire being blown into the forest, the Gospel spread like wildfire.

> *On that day a great persecution broke out against the church in Jerusalem, and all except the apostles were scattered throughout Judea and Samaria.* (Acts 8:1)

Listen. Hard times come. Grace killers will do their best to extinguish our freedom in Christ. As we loosen the tribal rules that have held the bride captive, not everyone will embrace her freedom. Some will fear faith without rules. Some will beg to be bound again. Perhaps it's best to burn the ropes of bondage holding faith hostage?

As rules fall and invitations extend, conflict will arise. Yet, don't we serve a God whose message is louder than adversity? His call to all is to be proclaimed beyond the walls, so when we see rules that keep others out, we must make the way clear so they can enter. When we witness leaders wavering—turning grace into a race of works—we cannot turn our head, for the Gospel is at stake.

And when the Lord turns your attention toward the mirror and you come face to face with your own tribal rules, you must let Him work through you so you continue to bear the fruit of grace which others find irresistible.

The Lord knows how to harness adversity. He brings glory to Himself through apparent tragedy. His will always reigns.

Father of Light, when night falls and hard times come, let me rest in the confidence that You're up to something. For I know Your Kingdom wastes nothing—that when I lose what is most precious to me, I gain what's most precious to You. Amen.

dance

Real slavery is living your life trying to gain favor; real freedom is knowing you already have favor. —Tullian Tchividjian

It's confession time. It's time to figure out if you're wired to march. Does the following statement ring true for you? **People around me think I'm committed to Jesus; but really, I've been committed to convincing others that I've got this religious life perfected. I've been marching—trying to win favor through performance and compliance.**

If the answer is yes, yes, and yes, then it is time to stop the march and start the dance. But how?

How do I learn to dance when all I've known is the stiff obedience to marching orders?

Let me tell you what worked for me:

- Stop trying.
- Start trusting.
- Repeat.

And then recognize that God has given some advantages—a learning curve, if you will—in these dance lessons.

> *"We who are Jews by birth and not sinful Gentiles know that a person is not justified by the works of the law, but by faith in Jesus Christ."* (Galatians 2:15-16a)

Paul is reminding the Galatians that they have the advantage of the law. For generations, their nation had followed the law, yet the law had never been able to save them. Jesus did the saving.

What was the advantage of having the law? To realize the law was no advantage.

Paul's words apply to another religious audience today—church people. So many times I have heard, "Pete, I grew up in church. I never met Jesus there and I never heard the Gospel." Yet I imagine that church was full of busy people—people busy trying to perform and please God. Busy being utterly exhausted—so tired that a person secretly wishes he or she could skip church just one Sunday and get some rest.

That's not a dancing church family. That's a marching church family. That's a family unaware of their advantage: They're free from performance.

Father, my need to perform has kept me from dancing. Show me something new to surrender each day—a new way to trust You. Help me learn to dance. Amen.

Fear is the passion of slaves. —Patrick Henry

Fear is rope that binds freedom. It's hard to dance when my feet are bound. It's hard to share a meal when my hands are tied. How can I follow when I'm unable to move?

People fear freedom because it's been taught that freedom leads to sin. This same teaching says that freedom and grace aren't gifts at all—but snares waiting to separate them from God.

And so they stand, feet together, arms at their sides, watching as others move and groove to the rhythm of God's grace.

What is so insane about this fear is that it's rooted in an unspoken belief that we can actually perform—or live—*in a manner that deserves God's approval.* **This fear whispers, "If you stand right here and march while those others are dancing, God's going to recognize your sober approach before His throne and will be more pleased with your marching than He is with their dancing."**

And just like that, I enter the arena of being my own savior and eradicate the need for Christ. Paul recognized this and was quick to set the record straight.

> *"By the works of the law no one will be justified."* (Galatians 2:16b)

Self-righteousness isn't going to make me acceptable to God. Marching isn't going to catch God's attention. **Standing firm and refusing to live life empowered and free by the Spirit of God is a form of self-inflicted suffering. This will not convince God of my holiness.**

If I am not justified by what I do—and if there isn't an award for refusing freedom—then who is stopping me from cutting the rope and living free?

I am.

Freedom doesn't lead to sin. Freedom is a gift from God, through Jesus. **The very idea that freedom leads to sin suggests that God gives gifts that inflict harm.** Nothing could be further from the truth.

Lord, I lift my bondage to You and ask You to cut the ropes of fear. Through the freedom of Your Spirit, I will praise You. Performance has been for my glory. Freedom is for Yours. I accept Your invitation to dance. Amen.

dance

I freed a thousand slaves. I could have freed a thousand more if only they knew they were slaves. —Harriet Tubman

Freedom releases us from fear. I am free from rejection. Free from condemnation. Free from judgment. Free!

Dance with me, friends.

Tullian Tchividjian writes in his book, *Jesus + Nothing = Everything,* "The gospel frees us to work and live from the secure basis of faith, not fear. We obey from the secure basis of grace, not guilt. And nothing could be more liberating."

The Gospel frees me to live life through the Spirit. I dance as if no one is watching—free from performing—and yet I dance knowing others are watching. May my dance be an invitation to join.

Paul wrote a letter to the young church in Corinth regarding their freedom:

> *"I have the right to do anything—but not everything is constructive. No one should seek their own good, but the good of others."* (1 Corinthians 10:23b-24)

He goes on to give permission to his readers to consume anything in the market without raising questions of conscience. Why? Because they were free. And their freedom, when intentionally lived out in practical, everyday situations, would invite others to dance.

Every day my life intertwines with others who don't recognize they're marching. So I dance. I dance freely, gracefully, and slowly—so that those who are watching can learn the steps.

May my love for You amplify the music of the dance so they can hear it from a distance and come running. I pray You will continue to teach me new steps so that I travel down new paths, extending the same invitation to new faces. Amen.

Anxiety is the dizziness of freedom. —Søren Kierkegaard

Modern Christianity has done a poor job of presenting grace.

I hear this often. "Grace is fine, but don't take it too far because then you'll fall into sin." This could also be spun, "Jesus is awesome, but don't trust Him too much because then you'll fall into sin."

Really? Jesus will lead us into sin? Or is it that He will lead us among the sinners? Look deeper in Galatians 2:17-18,

> *"But if, in seeking to be justified in Christ, we Jews find ourselves also among the sinners, doesn't that mean Christ promotes sin? Absolutely not! If I rebuild what I destroyed, then I really would be a lawbreaker."*

For the Jews—or church people—of Paul's day, to find themselves among the sinners meant sharing meals with them. This was law-breaking. This was dancing. This was unheard of before freedom through Christ. When I am justified—or set free—in Jesus, I will start dancing in ways I always believed were… well, "too free."

Perhaps then, if I am wondering whether or not I'm marching or dancing, I should take a look around me. Who are my fellow dancers? Do I find myself among the sinners? Are there freedoms around me causing me to lean deeper into the Spirit of God?

Or does everyone else on the dance floor dance just like I do?

One fear of freedom is that it will land us in a pit of sin. But Christ who is sinless and perfect has filled me with His Spirit. I live life through the Spirit. I dance in the Spirit. My freedom is surrendered to the Spirit. Thus, if I'm walking in the Spirit, I'm not walking in sin.

I can be sharing the dance floor with others whose freedom in Christ challenges my own.

Lord, I believe I can walk—yes, dance—in Your Spirit. Choreograph this dance for me! Guide my feet to Your music today as I move among those who need to see You. Open my eyes to the way You are moving through others. Is there something they can teach me about Your dance? Amen.

When I thought God was hard, I found it easy to sin; but when I found God so kind, so good, so overflowing with compassion, I smote upon my breast to think that I could ever have rebelled against One who loved me so…
—Charles Spurgeon

Everyone wearing white pants wants to jump in a mud pit. After all, this is why we bought the white pants—to trash them.

Absurd, right? (And a total waste of pants.)

So why do believers jump back into a cesspool of sin? And why do they—as they sit there in their muddy white pants—always give the same excuse, *I did it because I can. I'm free, remember? I can do this because grace covers it.*

It's okay to look down in their pit and say, "If that's what you think, you're totally missing grace."

Am I free to jump back into the cesspool of sin? Yes. Just as I'm free to put my hand on a hot stove or free to run my car into a tree. **I'm free to go back to filth. But why would I want to? Jesus rescued me from the filth. He pulled me out of the pit. He cleaned me off, gave me a new life, came to live inside me, and set me free to live.** I see nothing in the cesspool that is worth revisiting. Everything worth living for looks back at me from the eyes of Jesus.

> *What then? Shall we sin because we are… under grace? By no means! … Thanks be to God that, though you used to be slaves to sin, you have come to obey from your heart the pattern of teaching that has now claimed your allegiance. You have been set free from sin and have become slaves to righteousness.* (Romans 6:15, 17-18)

That word *allegiance* means I have taken the power I had—the freedom to choose sin—and I have chosen Jesus. I'm fully committed with no desire to turn back. I used to be a slave to sin, but everything has changed.

I'm not going back.

I will follow.

The cesspool will never again be my home, but there are still a lot of people who live there. People who need to hear the invitation to dance with their Savior.

I'm headed toward the pools of cess with You. Strengthen me, as there are old patterns there which once defined my life. Perhaps I don't trust myself, but I do trust You and the transformation You've done in me. I have a story to tell to those in cess—an invitation to extend—to those who live in those patterns of sin. Lead me. Amen.

I would maintain that thanks are the highest form of thought; and that gratitude is happiness doubled by wonder. —G. K. Chesterton

Happiness makes for great dancing posture. And for those of us who aren't happy, Amazon sells a "clavicle brace and posture support" so we can fake it.

I'm kidding.

That said, it doesn't take long to realize that I'm an incredible dancer when life is great. But life isn't always great. In fact, sometimes—more often than what's comfortable—life is hard.

By this point in the dance lessons, I've learned that to put on appearances is to march. I've traded in my marching boots for dancing shoes. I've abandoned a life driven by performance so I might live in abandon through the Spirit.

So the question arises: How can I dance beyond circumstances?

How can I dance with shoulders back and head high when heavy circumstances put a definite slump in my posture? Is there any hope beyond Amazon's clavicle brace?

Yes. Absolutely. The solution to dancing through life's circumstances is beautifully simple.

Give thanks.

> *Give thanks to the LORD, for he is good; his love endures forever.*
> (Psalm 118:1)

I know what you're thinking. *Pete, I just lost my job. My spouse just left. My house will be repossessed next month.* Or, *My child just said the most hurtful thing.*

I'm asking you. Try asking Jesus to be thankful through you today, no matter what. See what happens. **It's the ultimate perspective shifter as your focus shifts from circumstances to the Lord who is good and loves you forever.**

Father, I want to believe that I can dance through every circumstance, but some paralyze me. I thank You for Your Spirit who dwells in me and leads me too. May my list of gratitude be so lengthy that as I gaze toward the heavens, I lose my balance for one step, then two steps, and before I know it, I'm back in the dance again. Amen.

Heroes may not be braver than anyone else. They're just braver five minutes longer. —Ronald Reagan

Churches are filled with individuals who have experienced abuse at the hands of another. Cancer doesn't skirt the homes of believers. Loss occurs across faith boundaries. No, the church has its share of those who have lived through more than their share of evil and suffering.

God is good—really good—yet He doesn't seem to do everything in His power to keep us from suffering. So what does that make God? When bad things happen to His people, does it negate His goodness? If so, how can I dance with that kind of God?

Let's consider the American hero for a moment. The do-gooder who sweeps in at the last moment, saves the woman or child from danger, places them on solid ground, and then takes off again into the blue yonder.

He wears a cape. He protects people from harm. And then he leaves in a flash. Off to the next do-gooder task.

He's dressed to impress. He saves. And he leaves.

And he leaves.

The fundamental distinction between a human-fabricated hero and the Uncreated Father is found in the leaving. While God doesn't promise *easy*, He promises His *presence*.

He'll never take off into the blue yonder. Evil cannot scare Him away. He does not turn His head in our suffering. And it is His arms that break our fall in hard times. He is not a temporary hero; He is love.

> *Let Israel say: "His love endures forever."*
> *Let the house of Aaron say: "His love endures forever."*
> *Let those who fear the LORD say: "His love endures forever."*
> *When hard pressed, I cried to the LORD…*
>
> **The LORD is with me; I will not be afraid.** *What can mere mortals do to me?* (Psalm 118:2-6a, emphasis mine)

God Before me, Behind me, Around me, and In me—mere mortals can do a lot. It's the nature of abuse and oppression. But evil and suffering have stunted the growth of my trust abilities. Wrap me in Your presence the way a mother swaddles her child—tight, arms secured, so I can grasp nothing other than Your presence. Amen.

dance

Social networking is like a nightclub. Twitter is the dance floor, Tumblr is the bar, and Facebook is the people crying in the toilets. —Unknown

Some of our dance floors are just way too small. Yeah, Scripture calls us into wild, unbridled grace where we move freely in His Spirit. **Yet don't we all have limited vision and limiting expectations of God? Haven't we confined our dancing space by our circumstances?**

How many of us say, "If I can pay my bills, eat my meals, have my health, and raise children who flourish—oh, and keep my looks—then, *then,* I will dance."

Conditional, circumstantial dancing makes for a very small dance on a very small dance floor.

I've limited the space in which the Spirit can move in me.

Believers across the world live on less than three meals a day. Therefore, God's dance floor must be bigger than my food pyramid. And health? Since birth my body has been on a trajectory toward death. Wrinkles, malfunctions, and decreased productivity don't catch God by surprise. **Therefore, His dance floor extends beyond my limited tomorrows and into eternity.**

Remember, I'm not dancing to perform. I'm not dancing to earn God's approval. So if I can't pay my bills, I can still be dancing. If I get a bad bill of health, I can still be dancing. If my wife leaves and my dog dies and my truck won't go, I can still be dancing—or at least write a country and western song about it.

God doesn't promise an easy life, what our society calls "The Blessed Life." No, the true blessed life—the life that dances so freely that my feet never touch the same part of the dance floor twice—is found in Psalm 118:5:

> When hard pressed, I cried to the LORD; he brought me into a spacious place.

God is saying, "Come. Follow Me. Dance this way. You've been living in a tight place, afraid to breathe—waiting for the next shoe to drop. You've been trying to dance in an elevator, and I have the most incredible outdoor dance floor waiting for you."

Lord, Your Spirit gives the breath of life, and I admit I've been suffocating here. Lead me into this spacious place. A place where circumstances cannot bind me. A place where my arms spread wide to hug You before setting to spin, twirl, and dance before You. Amen.

This is the song that never ends. It goes on and on, my friends. Some people started singing it… —Norman Martin

Some things seem to go on forever (and we wish they wouldn't). Then there are things that do last forever—and we fear they won't.

God's love falls in the second category.

When Psalm 118 says, *"God's love endures forever,"* this is not just a figure of speech, nor is it wishful thinking. This is a quality of God's character explained in one beautiful Old Testament word: *hesed.*

Hesed tells the story of an unbreakable, unshakable bond between two parties. It is a love so deep that our language struggles to explain it. It is a covenant never retracted. Any offenses are covered by *hesed* mercy. It's a love in which forgiveness is rooted, and a love that has no end. If a wrong is committed against God, *hesed* is the place where His anger subsides in unlimited grace.

That's the sort of endurance God's love possesses.

That's the sort of love God *is*.

Why then, since God is for me because He's so in love with me, does He let me stumble on the dance floor? Why doesn't He just keep temptation and sin and difficult circumstances at arm's length—His arm's length?

God's love is not terminated when our feet get tripped up. In fact, like any good parent, God delights in watching His children learn the dance. Plus, there is always the hope that we'll turn to Him when we stumble.

In fact, God is more concerned with intimacy than He is fluency. With an ever-present God as a dance partner, when I stumble, it's certain that I'll fall into His arms. And this—this nearness and embrace—is the place He desires for His children.

Forever Father, nothing around me defines forever so that I can understand. Birth precedes death. Blossoms wilt. Beauty fades. Relationships fracture. Words break. But You've given me a forever love rooted in Your faithfulness and grace. While I don't fully comprehend, I hunger for it. And my appetite proves this love is real. Today, I pray for time to sit in Your presence and consider the depth of Your forever loving-kindness. Amen.

DAY 36

dance

When someone loves you, the way they say your name is different. You know that your name is safe in their mouth. —Jess C. Scott

Taking refuge in the wrong person can be awkward. If you've ever been jolted by a subway before securing your balance, you know what I mean. You go from standing to clinging in less than two seconds. Your apologies are muffled in an armpit, as your savior was smart enough to grab the monkey bar before takeoff. Ew.

As you smooth the suit and wonder whether that's Degree or Old Spice on the end of your nose, you realize that **some people just aren't the best places of refuge.**

In fact, they don't even appear to be glad you considered them a zone of safety.

Rough patches are going to come in life. What seems to be a smooth ride will suddenly jolt, and you'll lose your balance. As careers, finances, or relationships shatter, you're going to need a place of refuge—a place of safety and support.

How many times have I watched others take refuge in the wrong things?

There are so many people and places vying for our attention—claiming to have what we need. But only One knows what we need. He calls to us. He tells us to stop building our own place of refuge.

> *It is better to take refuge in the LORD than to trust in humans. It is better to take refuge in the LORD than to trust in princes.*
> (Psalm 118:8-9)

Why turn to a fellow traveler? Their journey is just as explosive as your own. Why turn to a person in power? Their power only comes from above.

Your dance partner is neither commoner nor prince. He is the Most High God. He has no beginning and no end. He is immune to circumstance, for circumstance is an occasion, an event marked by time. And your dance partner is eternal—unbound by the measurement He created.

There is no safer place to weather a storm than to be in a shelter immune to its fury.

Lord, I thank You that You've created me to look for a place of refuge—a relationship where I can put my confidence and trust. It's tempting to trust people I can see and hear. It's tempting to look to others of position and power, and place my trust in them. But Your Word says I can turn to You first. Not only that, but You are the better choice. Let me forever call You my home. Amen.

dance

He was no longer breathing, but his family was surprised by what the monitor showed. "The nurse said Dad was picking up Mom's heartbeat through Mom's hand. And we thought, 'Oh my gosh, Mom's heart is beating through him…' [Mom] died exactly an hour later." —"Couple Married 72 Years Dies Holding Hands," Christina Ng

There are more than a handful of stories from around the world that tell of couples who were married for decades and died within hours of each other. Their lives were so entangled that death could not separate them.

The children of these couples are struck with wonder as they consider the death of their parents evidence that neither could live without the other. Their death became one last act of love.

The Christian life is exactly this… well, except in reverse.

> *"I have been crucified with Christ and I no longer live, but Christ lives in me."* (Galatians 2:20)

At that moment of faith, when our fuzzy understanding of Jesus becomes hi-def and we decide we are all in, we are saved. We identify with Jesus as our Savior. In fact, through His Spirit, we identify with Him so strongly that we die with Him. **We are crucified with Christ and live by Christ. Our lives become entangled—no, more than entangled. His life becomes our life.**

It's the greatest love story ever told. It's tighter than tight. And it all starts with death.

Paul writes so that all will understand: **Identifying with Christ isn't part of the Christian life. It *is* the Christian's life.**

Lord, death can be terrifying until I realize that, with You, it brings life. Thank You for taking something shrouded in darkness and uncertainty, and making it the entry to light and life. Lead the way through death so that Christ lives in me. Amen.

dance

He thought her beautiful, believed her impeccably wise; dreamed of her, wrote poems to her, which, ignoring the subject, she corrected in red ink.
—Virginia Woolf

There's a secret to reading Scripture so it makes sense. Really, there is. If you are one of those who struggles to turn the pages because the Bible doesn't seem to make sense, this secret is for you:

Everything written before Jesus is pointing to Jesus. Everything written after Jesus is pointing to Jesus.

Jesus is the central subject in the Bible. So when we read a story about David or Noah or Isaiah, we can ask ourselves: *What is this telling me about God? How does this point toward Jesus?*

This same subject confusion can plague the Christian life. I can get caught up in: *Where am I supposed to go? Who am I supposed to serve? What am I supposed to care about?*

These aren't bad questions. But the subject of each is all wrong. **Life in Christ isn't about accolades and accomplishments. It's about Jesus alive in me.**

Paul is writing to the church in Galatia, and essentially to all of us, and he's telling us how to live this life in Christ. It's his personal statement of faith, and it sounds something like this:

- I'm dead.
- I'm indwelt.
- I'm depending.

> *"I have been crucified with Christ… **I'm dead**… and I no longer live, but Christ lives in me. **I'm indwelt.** The life I now live in the body, I live by faith in the Son of God… **I'm depending.**"* (Galatians 2:20, additions and emphasis mine)

Here are some better questions: *Who is my strength? Who is my love? Who is the overflow of grace in my life?* The answer is simple. It isn't Pete. It's Jesus.

God Whose Spirit lives in me, I've been trying to live as the star of my own show, and I'm exhausted. Instead, I long to follow the example of that first star the night You came to earth. Let Your Spirit shine in me and point to You. Amen.

dance

I'd rather die my way than live yours. —Lauren Oliver

The Bible says we are dead. That's kind of creepy. It doesn't sound like the "Good News" everybody needs to hear. But actually, it's one of the most amazing, powerful truths in God's Word: We were crucified with Christ and we've died. But what have we died to? That's the question. What have we left behind? (It's certainly not the capacity to sin. As of this morning, I was still capable!)

> *"For through the law I died to the law so that I might live..."*
> (Galatians 2:19)

Whether we realize it or not, whether we act on it or not, we are dead to the laws of performance-based acceptance. We are dead to the notion that we can do anything to earn additional favor from God. That's powerful! With clarity, we can embrace the truth that only Jesus can do what we never could.

Somehow, in some way, when Jesus died on the cross, we did too. Reaching across time, our souls cried out in anguish—the same anguish as Jesus on that cross—and right there, on the cross, we released our last breath and said so long to a life of our dizzying need to perform and *do it all for God's sake.*

And oh, this death serves a most beautiful purpose.

"So that..." When I read this tiny transitional phrase in Scripture, my eyes are peeled for purpose. For what purpose did I die to the law? For what purpose did I try to stop gaining God's favor through ritual and performance? *"So that I might live."*

Friend, in my new life—filled with His breath—I am calling to all the exhausted, to all the marchers whose boots are so heavy with mud and muck from the cesspool of sin. I am calling to *you* to leave the boots in the mud and approach Him with bare feet dancing.

You are on the most sacred of dance floors.

Leave the boots behind, my friend. Leave them in the pile of funeral attire.

Die and live.

Giver of Life, what an invitation! What an exchange. You are calling me to leave behind a life of rules and "not enoughs" so You can give me a life of acceptance and "more than enoughs." I accept. Wholeheartedly, I accept death. It's what I've been waiting for—a call to live. Amen.

The more we get what we now call "ourselves" out of the way and let Him take us over, the more truly ourselves we become… He made [us] all. He invented—as an author invents characters in a novel—all the different [people] that you and I were intended to be… It is when I turn to Christ, when I give myself up to His Personality, that I first begin to have a real personality of my own. —C. S. Lewis

It's not easy trying to explain to children that Christ lives in their hearts. Undoubtedly, there is always that literal child who wants to know how Christ fits there. Why did He choose her heart and not her ears so she can hear Him? Can He cause her heart to explode? As I try to explain all the complications of a heart-dweller, I end up entering into a theological conversation far above her level. She walks away perplexed. And I walk away amazed.

Because that child was right. Jesus doesn't live in her heart. That's taking the incredible gift of the Holy Spirit and compressing it, compacting it to manageable size.

The essence of indwelling is that Jesus, the second person of the Trinity, indwells us—lives in me—through the Holy Spirit, the third person of the Trinity.

The Creator indwells my spirit, influences my soul, and impacts my body…

> *"And I no longer live, but Christ lives in me."* (Galatians 2:20)

The Greek for *in* means to rest and settle down. Paul could have chosen another Greek word, *eis*, which means to move into, but he didn't. He chose *en*. If you are in Christ, then Christ is in you. His Spirit has come to *rest* in you. He's *settled* in you. *God Himself lives in you.*

This is reconciliation so complete it's unity. Can your mind understand the implications? You never again have to ask for help as though Jesus and you were two separate entities. You are one. His life is your life. You persevere in His strength. You love with His love.

And in Him, You have found yourself. And as it turns out, you resemble a little of your Father.

Lord, not only do You live in me, but You love me. You want to settle here. You call me home. What grace! Fill me to full and overflowing, Lord, so I spill this grace onto those around me. So all will know there's no containing You. Amen.

DAY 41

We were together. I forget the rest. —Walt Whitman

What's the secret to avoiding burnout? Stop trying to be Jesus.

You laugh, but it's true. I've been in ministry for a number of years. I've seen people work themselves to the bone. They pour themselves out past empty and then turn themselves inside out. They do it all for Jesus. They do it all for love. Their intentions are purehearted but their methodology is unbiblical.

If you want to avoid burnout, you're going to have to let Jesus be Jesus—and that requires a great deal of surrender and dependence.

> *"This is what the kingdom of God is like. A man scatters seed on the ground. Night and day, whether he sleeps or gets up, the seed sprouts and grows, though he does not know how. All by itself the soil produces grain…"* (Mark 4:26-28)

The Kingdom of God is like this:

- God grows it.
- God produces it.
- God knows how it works.

The Kingdom of God is like this: You don't have to kill yourself to make sure it lasts. You are able to abide in the Lord and scatter where He tells you to scatter, plant where He tells you to plant, and—this is amazing—rest at regular intervals in between.

If the indwelling is the Spirit's resting in you, then dependence is you resting in Him.

It's that simple and yet that hard.

A little countercultural prescription for the day: Dependency means we wait for God to do His thing without doing it for Him. And in the waiting, we can just enjoy His company. (Big sigh.)

Lord, I thank You that I don't have to do this by myself. You've given me a specific role: I must abide in You and You abide in me. I don't have to know the inner workings of Your Kingdom and its growth. I don't have to have all the answers. All I need is You, so that I can scatter Your truth in lives around me. Amen.

DAY 42

When Christ calls a man, he bids him come and die. —Dietrich Bonhoeffer

Let me share a little unsolicited advice in dating and relationships. You should never invite someone into a relationship with the words, "I love you. Come die." It might have worked for Romeo and Juliet, but I'm certain Shakespeare squeezed the only ounce of romance from that line. I mean, think about it:

I love you. Come die.

Not exactly painting a portrait of a bright future. Not very high on the scale of warm fuzzies. Coming from the wrong person, it would likely cause you to reach for your phone and call the police. But from Jesus, "I love you. Come die," is not a threat. It's an amazing invitation to *live.*

Listen, it's one thing to be exposed to Jesus. Many people are exposed to Jesus. Some like what they see, while others don't. Some are drawn to His Church, while others are repelled. Some choose to believe, while others hesitate or even refuse. **But it's something entirely different to realize you are dead and Christ lives in you.**

> *"I have been crucified with Christ and I no longer live, but Christ lives in me."* (Galatians 2:20)

Let this soak in for a moment. We were taken to the cross with Jesus, and died there. By trusting in Him, that death is applied to us, and the resurrection is as well. It's amazingly powerful to realize that Christ *lives—is living, is acting, is leading, is* life *in me.*

I love you. Come die… *and you will find life.*

It's an invitation and revelation from God's own Spirit that changes the course of our lives. It changes the essence of who we are. I am no longer Pete. Doing things for Pete. Living life for Pete. Serving God with Pete's own efforts. But God's Word and His Spirit call us into a deeper, more profound existence:

> *"For **whoever wants to save their life** will lose it, but whoever loses their life for me will find it."* (Matthew 16:25, emphasis mine)

We've died to a life defined by self and we're alive to Christ. In short, the Son of God indwells us. Isn't that incredible?

Lord, I've been trying to save my life, when, in Your love, I died with You and You filled me with Your life. You've been alive in me all along. Lord, I praise You that I don't need more strength. You are my strength. I don't need to chase after Your Spirit. Your Spirit is in me. I collapse before You today as one who is dead to self and alive through You. Please show me one new way You wish to live through me today. Amen.

dance

To die is to be with the Lord. It is not just an idea; it is a reality.
—Francis Schaeffer

"She's with Jesus now. We can have comfort that she's dancing with Jesus as we speak…" Have you ever heard that at a funeral? Probably. Me too… because as a pastor, I'm probably the one saying it. It's not that this isn't true; it's that it's not the whole truth. It's that the timing is wrong. The good news isn't just that the dead person is now alive with Christ. It's that our dancing and living in unity with Christ begins long before our physical death.

> *"And I will ask the Father, and he will give you another advocate to help you and be with you forever—the Spirit of truth… you know him, for he lives with you and will be in you. … Because I live, you also will live. On that day you will realize that I am in my Father, and you are in me, and I am in you." (John 14:16-17, 19b-20)*

Scripture says I died with Christ 2,000 years ago on a hill outside Jerusalem. As a little boy, I received Jesus' free gift of salvation, and that death was applied to me. He then indwelled me by His Spirit, giving me His Life. Thus, He's dwelled in me since the age of four. It's not an idea or a romanticized notion. It's a reality. I died, and I've been "with the Lord" every moment ever since. Sure, it's going to change when I shed this creaky body and can relate to Him "face to face" on a purely spiritual level. But the fact that He is *already* in me is the mystery, and the joy, and the unique truth of the Christian message.

Isn't that beautiful? Perhaps you've never thought of it before—that you don't have to wait until eternity to live in Christ and Christ in you. Perhaps you thought it was far off in the future—only a reality through death.

But the good news is this: It's now.

- What God does, He does through you.
- Who God is, He is through you.

You're not a little god. No. The news is better than that. You are filled with God. You've always been made in His image; but upon belief, that image becomes living color.

I hope the words spoken at my funeral include, "Now there is a man who's been with Jesus, dancing and living, for almost nine decades." And I pray they say that about you too.

Indwelling God, I believe that You are in me and live in me. But it's a reality that's hard to wrap my mind around. In Your wisdom, lift the veil over my mind that keeps me from understanding how Your indwelling changes everything about life here on earth. I want to dance with You now, live with You now, walk with You today. Amen.

dance

I went to a bookstore and asked the saleswoman, "Where's the self-help section?" She said if she told me, it would defeat the purpose. —George Carlin

God helps those who help themselves, right? Well, not exactly. Actually, not even close. The bookstore does have a complete "self-help" section telling us we're supposed to survive life's toughest seasons by our own strength—that we're in this alone. But nothing could be further from the truth. The truth is much more powerful, much more profound, and much more incredible:

> *His divine power has given us everything we need for a godly life through our knowledge of him who called us by his own glory and goodness.*
> (2 Peter 1:3)

Everything we need to live a godly life comes through knowing Him. Don't get me wrong. Peter doesn't promise life will be easy or carefree. He does say that we have everything we need to not just survive— but thrive—in a life that experiences Christ.

> *Through these [Jesus] has given us his very great and precious promises, so that through them you may participate in the divine nature…* (2 Peter 1:4)

What? We can "participate in the divine nature" in His glory and goodness —because we have everything needed to live a godly life through Christ? Is it possible that through the presence of Jesus' Spirit in us, we are *that* close, *that* intimate with Him right here, right now?

This is powerful Scripture. God's power has given us everything we need to live as He wishes:

- We don't have to pray for strength. Jesus is our strength.
- We don't have to struggle to love people. He loves through us.
- We don't have to wait for joy. He is our joy.

No, we don't need to help ourselves. We lack nothing. Why? Because God lives in us.

That's truth. And "self-help" is a faint and deceptive endeavor.

God with me, I thought I was doing this alone and that somehow I could make my life something worthy of Your love. I kept working on myself, preparing myself for You—like a person still rushing around cleaning the house and changing sheets after company has arrived. And You've watched, waiting, calling me to be still so I might enjoy Your presence in my home. Jesus, calm me. Show me that I don't need to work or fight alone anymore. I praise You that You've given me everything I need. Will You unwrap the gifts and show me how to experience Your life? Amen.

DAY 45

dance

The Christ within who is our hope of glory is not… a hobby, a part-time project, a good theme for a book, or a last resort when all human effort fails. He is our life, the most real fact about us. He is the power and wisdom of God dwelling within us. —Brennan Manning

Does Christ in me change anything? Absolutely.

- Since Jesus is in us, we can truly experience life. Not just experiencing any life—*the* life of Christ. Far beyond salaries, pensions, and square footage. Far beyond fertility, infertility, loss, and success. We experience the fullness of the life of Christ *because He is in us.*

- Since Jesus is in us, we can experience life with endurance. When we feel worn out, we can keep going. When our patience feels depleted, we can still love well *because He is in us.*

- Since Christ is in us, we can say no to sin. If we are in Christ, sin is temporary insanity. It is not who we are. It's not where we belong. We've died to indwelling sin and are alive in Christ *because He is in us.*

- And as we allow Him to live through us, our lives will matter *because He is in us.*

"I am the vine; you are the branches. If you remain in me and I in you, you will bear much fruit; apart from me you can do nothing." (John 15:5)

For hungry souls starving to find purpose, this changes everything. We desire to make our lives count. We desire purpose and legacy. With Jesus in us, we are promised that our life will offer nourishment to others.

So let me ask you, does being indwelt by God change anything? No, not just anything—everything: I was dead, now I live. I was tired, now I persevere. I was defeated, now I'm victorious. I was consumed by self, now I offer nourishment for others.

But even more than that, I'm participating in the divine life. It's the closest intimacy with God available here on earth. I'm never alone. I'm always able—*because He is in me…* and if you've opened your heart to Him and let Him in, He is in you too.

Jesus, thank You for making my heart, mind, body, and soul Your home. I'm like the rough-hewn manger carrying the world's most precious treasure—You! I've been handling Your indwelling like an electrical current, turning my surrender on and off like a switch. Today, in a new way, I ask that You would make me aware of the truth about Your constant presence and power in me. Here I am, Lord. I'm ready to experience Your life. Amen.

dance

Let no one ever come to you without leaving better and happier. Be the living expression of God's kindness: kindness in your face, kindness in your eyes, kindness in your smile. —Mother Teresa

I met a kid while playing basketball some time ago. He was new, and I noticed him mostly because he was so much younger than the rest of us there. As we were wrapping up the game, he said he wouldn't be back next week—he had to get the kids to school.

He—a kid—had to get kids to school.

It turns out that he was a Christian. When newly wed, he and his wife decided to take in two teenage kids who were struggling. One had special needs, and the other was having a difficult time. Neither was in an environment that nurtured their growth and health, so this young man and his wife decided to take them in.

"Wow!" I said, after he shared how the kids were excelling. "What do you want to do with your life?"

"Well, I love these kids to death. They're beautiful kids. I want to get these kids through high school, and then I want to go to med school."

A young man putting dreams on hold because he's in love with two struggling teens?

That's evidence of the indwelling Christ. And when you start recognizing this truth—that Christ indwells us—you start seeing the life of Christ in people all around you.

- They are willing to put dreams aside so they can care for others.
- They are willing to let go of time and resources so that one more person's needs might be met.
- They are willing to let go of the temporal in order to experience Christ.
- They are heroes—both sung and unsung throughout history.

And yet, for those who bow their knee to Jesus, we know it's not really them at all. No, not them, but Christ in them—dancing, serving, and loving others just as He can do through us all.

He Who is Greater, I want to do what Your Spirit does, love as Your Spirit loves, sacrifice as Your Son sacrificed. I want my life to matter to someone other than myself. I can't do this, but You can. Because You've grafted me into Your life and Your Kingdom, I ask that You will. Open my eyes to see what You see. Live through me today as a living expression of who You are, Jesus. Amen.

dance

The reason why many are still troubled, still seeking, still making little forward progress is because they haven't yet come to the end of themselves.
—A. W. Tozer

Death is the beginning of life.

I know that sounds crazy, but a lot of things in Christianity sound crazy—and I'm not even talking about physical death leading to eternal life. I'm talking about dying to the law so you can live right now.

> *"Through the law I died to the law so that I might live for God."*
> (Galatians 2:19)

The word *for* isn't in the original Greek. The verse literally says, "so that I might live God." Wow. Think about that. **Something powerful happens when we abandon all our petty religious rules. We are set free for something bigger when we quit trying to please God while living for ourselves.** What did Paul say?

I died to the law—to the rules that have dictated my living—*so that* I might live God.

What does it look like to "live God"?

- It isn't mandatory quiet time every day. It's freedom from guilt and freedom to engage with God all the time.

- It isn't perfect adherence to the Ten Commandments. It's peace that God has my best interests in mind, and I can trust Him to guide me moment by moment.

- It isn't to-the-penny tithing of 10 percent. It's giddy generosity inspired by the Spirit, and the awareness that everything belongs to God.

- It's not about your political party. It's seeing people the way God sees them and releasing the need to be correct.

Ultimately, it is always about letting Jesus live in and through us!

No, "living God" isn't marching within the confines of a bunch of rules. It's dancing within the current of ever-flowing love. That's the dance of grace He invites you to—and that's an invitation worth dying for.

Giver of Life, I've tried so many methods of resuscitation for this dry soul. Nothing satisfies. Make my life in the Spirit new and different today. Lead me away from the rules, and show me Your way of living, one step at a time. Amen.

Criticism may not be agreeable, but it is necessary. It fulfills the same function as pain in the human body; it calls attention to the development of an unhealthy state of things. —Winston Churchill

I heard of a guy who is a musician by passion and a music teacher by trade. One day I was sitting in his foyer when a student came in for lessons. Minutes later I heard a few notes of melody followed by a horrific noise. A few more notes and another horrific noise.

I got up to peek around the corner and see what was going on. Every time the student struck a wrong note, the teacher would imitate the sound of a buzzer.

BZZZZ! Wrong! BZZZZ! Wrong! BZZZZ! Wrong!

Living the law is like living beneath a buzzer all the time. All those rules. All the effort. All the paranoia. And before we know it, we're not even ourselves anymore.

Eventually, living under the law demands that we live in hiding. We can't let anyone see how messy we are—and as a result, we become pretenders on the outside. "Oh yeah, I'm just great." "The Lord spoke to me fifty different ways this week, once for each time I prayed!" "After I complete these Sabbath duties, I'm going to calculate my volunteer hours this month!"

But inside we know better, don't we? The rules criticize us daily and we know we're failing.

> *Therefore no one will be declared righteous in God's sight by the works of the law; rather, through the law we become conscious of our sin.* (Romans 3:20)

Please understand, the law's job is to make you conscious of your sin. And that's a good thing. **But today when you hear the buzzer, you have a choice: You can stay enslaved—marching beneath the buzzer. Or you can seek out an alternative—freedom in grace,** for

> *All are justified freely by his grace through the redemption that came by Christ Jesus.* (Romans 3:24)

Let this truth soak into your dry and weary soul: **You are accepted—failures and all—through Jesus.** May that nagging failure always drive you toward grace.

Lord, thank You that I no longer try to earn my keep in eternity. I don't need to hide my inadequacies. Show me where I'm guilty of nagging—of being that buzzer in the lives of others. Teach me to speak the life that comes from Your free grace. Amen.

The only way to deal with an unfree world is to become so absolutely free that your very existence is an act of rebellion. —Albert Camus

Some people can't handle freedom. Some don't know what to do with it and it makes them nervous. Others express anger and judgment when, in fact, they are dying from jealousy. They want that freedom for themselves, but they aren't confident that Christ really unlocked the door to their cell.

Question: How can we love these people whose envy is the root of their disdain for us?

Answer: We can show them the way of the Spirit.

> *But the fruit of the Spirit is love, joy, peace, forbearance, kindness, goodness, faithfulness, gentleness and self-control. Against such things there is no law. Those who belong to Christ Jesus have crucified the flesh with its passions and desires. Since we live by the Spirit, let us keep in step with the Spirit.* (Galatians 5:22-25)

A life lived in the Spirit with this fruit is something everyone wants to taste.

Our lives can be so radically different and make Christ so incredibly attractive that they are drawn to Him in us, like moths to light. This happens. We see it all through the Gospels. These Pharisees and teachers of the law are so against Jesus and everything He's teaching, and yet there they are, in every scene. They truly believe everything Jesus is saying is wrong—blasphemy, rebellious—and yet they can't stop listening. They can't stop coming.

He's attractive to them and they hate it.

In the end, they tried to kill the rebellion, never realizing that Jesus' death is like inserting the key. And His resurrection flung open the door so that every single person who hears and believes is free—free to live that same radical, rebellious life of freedom—a life so bright it's attractive to the most skeptical.

Lord, please make my life look radically different from what they are expecting—make it so different today that my life looks like You, not me. Your Spirit is a beautiful choreographer. Let me keep in step so that others are captivated by the dance. Amen.

DAY 50

dance

And now the sequence of events in no particular order... —Dan Rather

Sequence matters. If we get the order of things mixed up, everything gets messed up. Just ask a cook or a mechanic. Same thing goes in our dance with Christ.

In our spiritual life, if we get things in the wrong order, we might live with the idea that we have two natures that are in conflict: who we used to be versus who we are now in Jesus. A good dog and a bad dog fighting inside of us for control of our soul. Under legalistic teaching, it becomes our job to tame the bad one— our old self.

But this is not what the New Testament teaches, friends. We can't skip the sequence; sequence matters. Galatians 2:20 shows us the order:

- *"I have been crucified with Christ and I no longer live."* The old self, the old nature is history, past tense, done with. Who you once were died on the cross with Jesus.
- *"But Christ lives in me."* The bad has been replaced by the best. The Spirit of Jesus lives inside you now—He is active and present in you. Incredible, yet true!
- *"The life I now live in the body, I live by faith in the Son of God, who loved me and gave himself for me."* This is when you begin to participate in what God has already done through Jesus. *Now* you live by faith, by trusting what God has already done and what Christ will do through you.

We simply trust because we have died with Him and are indwelt by Him. It's a beautiful relationship—a dance of dependence upon Jesus and His Spirit to live through us.

But remember, the sequence matters. Otherwise, you will find yourself trying to live by faith and trust according to your own strength, and this isn't possible. This is bondage—trying to live like Christ without the strength and character of Christ living through us.

Lord, I've been living this life of faith my way. I've come to You on my terms and announced to You my sin and my plan to eradicate it from my own life. No wonder I continuously fall short. No wonder I feel like such a failure. Sequence matters. I ask that You would ingrain the proper order in my mind so I can live it today. Please renew my thinking. I've been forgetting the order: I've died with Christ. I'm home to your Spirit. By Your grace, I will live in faith simply because it is a fruit of that same Spirit! Thank You for this freedom. Amen.

Faith combined with hope grows into trust. —Brennan Manning

Honestly, deep down inside, don't we all search for the magic formula that will get us what we want? The quirky ritual that makes our team score. The right calculation that will give us winning lottery numbers. The right actions that will make people love us. The right prayers that will twist God's arm to get Him to do what we want. Yeah, honestly, we search for the formulas, don't we? But there's really only one formula I know that works every time.

Faith + hope = trust.

That's the equation for life.

Faith can be simply defined as bringing everything to Jesus, being honest about our hopes, and trusting in Him for all things. Period. This formula will save you. We see it played out in Scripture sometimes. Consider the desperate dad of a boy possessed by a violent demonic spirit. He brought his son to Jesus and cried out an honest request:

> *"But if you can do anything, take pity on us and help us."*
>
> *"'If you can'?" said Jesus. "Everything is possible for one who believes."*
>
> *Immediately the boy's father exclaimed, "I do believe; help me overcome my unbelief!"* (Mark 9:22-24)

His trust was so-so and his hope weak. Yet in faith, he brought his desire to Jesus seeking healing.

Faith is bringing everything to Jesus. Faith + hope = trust. What do you need to bring to Him right now?

Father, I've spent years trying to pump up my own faith so that when I pray, I can pray with confidence. The truth is I believed this confidence would get me what I want. Father, I'm ready to stop trying and start bringing. In fact, this prayer is the first step. I bring to You my misunderstanding of faith. May Your complete knowledge abound in me. Amen.

True faith rests upon the character of God… —A. W. Tozer

Jesus doesn't work harder for those who try harder. So if you've been busy muscling up some stellar faith, hoping someday you'd have just enough to have just a little more Jesus, you can stop.

Jesus isn't concerned about the quantity or quality of your faith. He just desires to be the object of your faith.

> *"The life I now live in the body, I live by faith in the Son of God..."*
> (Galatians 2:20)

When we depend upon someone other than Jesus, we are going to be disappointed. Our society offers a buffet of choices: health and wellness, dead people, spouses, careers, IRAs, and even pastors. All of them are imperfect and totally unqualified to become the object of your faith.

How about today's gurus? They're simply preaching secular legalism—teaching a different list of rules, but rules all the same. Rules can't hold you up.

I remember my elementary school science teacher explaining the human skeleton. If all went well, I'd never see my own bones. But without them, I'd be nothing more than a blob of flesh and muscle on the pavement. Same goes with faith. People are always looking for a visible object of faith. Yet, it's the ascended Christ and the invisible but indwelling Spirit who hold us up in this faith journey.

In fact, Scripture teaches that faith is produced by God's Spirit in us. We have no control over its volume and quantity in our lives. But we do get to choose whom we trust.

What are you facing today? In whom or in what will you put your faith?

Almighty God, I've been taught to choose my words wisely, lest I speak words void of faith. I've been taught to pray using certain methods and words, lest I forget to say the right thing the right way. I've been taught every spiritual manipulation, and none of them stood a chance of manipulating You. Starting today, renew my mind so that I might think thoughts rooted in the mind of Christ. Renew my words so they are life. Hold me up in faith and lead me in the dance. Amen.

dance

Prayer is not asking. Prayer is putting oneself in the hands of God, at His disposition, and listening to His voice in the depth of our hearts.
—Mother Teresa

It's one thing to know about faith; it's another to live by faith. How do we depend on Jesus in everyday life?

- Deliver the burden to God.
- Rest in Him.
- Depend on Him.
- And then do what He says in the power of the Spirit.

That's it? That's it.

Most of us can make it through the first three but get stuck on the last one. The big question is always: How do I know what Jesus is saying to me?

God communicates however He desires, but starting with Scripture is always a good idea. We can also listen to friends and mentors—making sure to take their advice back to the Bible to see if it parallels.

He desires to communicate and has given His Spirit to guide you. Take your burden to Him. Trust that He knows. Depend upon Him for the resolution. And then act when you're led to do so. That's the beginning of great stories.

I once sat next to a couple who were in their 50s. He was a college professor and she was working in retail. Both had been burdened for their city and had taken that burden to God. "It's hard for the incarcerated," the wife told me. "When they are released, they suddenly no longer live in community and are often totally alone." In faith, the couple continued working their jobs and trusted that He'd let them know when it was time to do something. When we met, they were six months away from moving into a new transitional community. "Our home will be a healthy, faith-filled community for them. We won't give them a chance to feel alone."

That's just one story of one couple who delivered the burden to God, rested in Him, depended on Him, and then did what He said in the power of the Spirit.

This is the adventure of the Christian life, friends—where life gets excitingly out of our hands. What's He doing in your story?

Lord, I can barely contain myself. The fact that You desire to give me guidance and lead me in an adventure of faith is more than I can handle. Let's get started right now, Lord. I've been struggling. I'm turning this over to You and am going to wait for You to lead me. I'm depending upon You because You are faithful. Now I'm listening for You because You speak. Amen.

dance

You are really and truly and completely free. There is no kicker. There is no if, and, or but. You are free. You can do it right or wrong. You can obey or disobey. You can run from Christ or run to Christ… You can cry, cuss, and spit, or laugh, sing, and dance… You're free… really free. —Steve Brown

Life often presents two different types of choices: There is the either-or choice, where you can choose one thing *or* the other—but you can't choose both. Then there is the both-and choice, which are actually two separate decisions. You can choose both this *and* you can choose that—*and* you can have them both at the same time.

When it comes to freedom in the Spirit and legalism, Jesus presents us with a black and-white, one way or the other, either-or decision. No two ways about it. We have two legitimate choices, but we are going to have to choose between them.

We are, in fact, dead to sin—we don't have to choose to be so each morning. We are "in the Spirit" by default—we don't have to choose to be so. That's biblical truth. But we do get to choose whether we will live according to these truths (by walking in the Spirit), or whether we are going to let ourselves be placed under the law and live a lie (by marching in the strength of our flesh).

The choice is yours. You can either be a dancer or a marcher, but you can't be both. You either dance in the Spirit or march in the power of your own flesh.

The book of Romans is almost entirely committed to this either-or decision, and Paul makes it absolutely clear which is the true way to go.

> *Therefore, there is now no condemnation for those who are in Christ Jesus, because through Christ Jesus the law of the Spirit who gives life has set you free from the law of sin and death.* (Romans 8:1-2)

So, what are you going to do today? It's either law or grace! **Are you going to accept Jesus' invitation to dance and live freely in His Spirit moment by moment?** Or will you subject yourself to the drill sergeant of legalism and try to flesh it out as best you can?

Lord, the marching boots stomping around me are so loud, I haven't been able to hear the music of Your Spirit. My gracious Lord, today, in the authoritative truth of Your Word, I put on the dancing shoes of your Spirit—the ones that are light, fit perfectly, and are ready to follow Your lead in all things. Please, give me ears to hear Your music. Amen.

dance

Jesus invited us to a dance and we've turned it into a march of soldiers, always checking to see if we're doing it right and are in step and in line with the other soldiers. —Steve Brown

Some time ago, I was watching a cross-country running race. Individuals from several high schools running their hearts out mile after mile. The leader, a kid who had maintained a strong lead throughout the course, was distancing himself from the pack. His stride was long and fluid—you could tell he was a natural runner. But as they rounded the curve on the last half-mile, he gave in to the temptation to check himself against the others, to see how he was doing. He turned his head, taking his eyes off the path before him, and looked back over his shoulder. Sure enough—it was almost in slow motion—his foot caught on a tree root at just the wrong time. His rhythm was thrown off. His stride crumpled. He stumbled and ended up losing his lead.

Any good running coach will tell you one of the keys to running the best race: Don't look back.

Life in the body of Christ can be the same. Many of us have grown up marching. We've been marching for years—one marcher among thousands. When we look to our left, there's marching. To our right? More marching. There have been marchers before us and behind us.

And then we hear the invitation to dance. Swept away by the music of the Spirit and the Word, at first we only have eyes for our dance partner. We're learning the steps of the Spirit. We're whirling in our freedom.

And then time passes. We start to look around. We compare our dancing to those around us who are still marching. We start to feel self-conscious. Is it possible we made a mistake? Absolutely not.

> As we have already said, so now I say again: If anybody is preaching to
> you a gospel other than what you accepted, let them be under God's curse!
> Am I now trying to win the approval of human beings, or of God?
> (Galatians 1:9-10a)

There is only one Gospel, one invitation to be free. Keep looking ahead, running in the Spirit according to the Truth of God's Word. Legalism—like a tree's roots—is waiting to trip you up. Don't look back.

God, my thoughts get jumbled when I look around and see people I love still marching. But Your Word says I have the mind of Christ. There is one Gospel, one resurrection, whose promise dwells inside me. May Your wisdom forever guide me in the dance, away from lies that will trip me up. Amen.

Under the law, even the best failed. Under grace, even the worst can be saved!
—Joseph Prince

Choices, choices, choices. We usually like them. What do I want on my burger? What should I do this weekend? And most of us like to keep our options open. Why limit yourself to one way when you could do it all? Okay, cheese *and* mayo on the burger, and let's have a barbeque while we swim at the lake…

Sure, some things in life offer us simultaneous options. But what if I told you that you had to choose between the cross of Christ and the Ten Commandments? This is awkward, isn't it? We tend to think of this as a both-and decision, but it's really either-or.

We have salvation—the free gift from God's grace. And then we have sanctification—our spiritual growth. We're good with our salvation being completely God, but then many get confused and insist spiritual growth is a result of our own effort. They aren't sure where to start… so they usher in the law.

It's as though they're saying, "God, Your Spirit has served its purpose. We'll take it from here. After all, we have this list of do's and don'ts to guide us."

Right?

Wrong.

> *I am astonished that you are so quickly deserting the one who called you to live in the grace of Christ and are turning to a different gospel—which is really no gospel at all.* (Galatians 1:6-7a)

That different Gospel was one that included human effort and strict adherence to the law. Moses didn't hold the Gospel—he held the law, once beautiful in its time but now fulfilled. **Today, in the shadow of the cross, He calls us to walk in the Spirit—in an intimate, willful following of the living Word that guides us.** Jesus was all about this. Over and over again, He presented the choice: Who is it going to be, Me or Moses? Trusting or working? Either the Gospel is enough, or it isn't.

Yes, you can have it both ways with your burger. But when it comes to God, you can either choose the cross or you can choose the law.

Gracious Savior, I choose one God and one Gospel. I choose one way of living and that is through Christ and by Your Spirit. Open my hands to release the old so I can hold tightly to this new Life of grace! Amen.

Moral #1: If you work hard, stay focused, and never give up, you will eventually get what you want in life.

Moral #2: Sometimes the things we want most in life are the things that will kill us. —Donald Miller

The word *bewitched* is used only once in all of the New Testament. It means "to be fixated upon something that is going to destroy you." The phrase "deer in the headlights" is appropriate here. Here in Texas, that's a common occurrence. And as the truck bears down on the staring doe, the deer never wins. Paul saw the Galatians were doing just this, and he pleaded for them to turn around.

> *You foolish Galatians! Who has bewitched you? Before your very eyes Jesus Christ was clearly portrayed as crucified.* (Galatians 3:1)

The Christian life is trusting not working, and yet, some work so hard. Taking their eyes off the cross, they are dazed again by the bewitching lights of the law. They charge ahead in their efforts, alone, leaving the Spirit of God behind. Perhaps they don't realize they are headed for destruction, for what is the Christian life without the Spirit of God leading?

You foolish Galatians! Like a father whose child just ran into the street and narrowly missed being hit by a car, Paul is pulling the Galatians back into his arms—chastising them in love. *Don't do that again! Have you forgotten what I told you? You could have gotten hurt! Worse, you could have been killed!*

It isn't the desire for transformation that most often goes wrong; it's our execution of that desire. When we take the Christian life by the reins and start leading it ourselves, we get ahead of God. We prioritize our wants above God's wants. We work hard, but we trust little.

There's an alternative: **Stay focused on the cross.** Allow God to set the pace. Follow His lead at every intersection. **It's hard for a child to dart into the street when he or she is holding the hand of a loving father.**

Lord, I live in a society that trains me to set my own pace or get trampled. Have I entered into Your Kingdom with that same mentality? Renew my mind today! As Your child, I give You my hand to hold. Show me Your pace. Lead me… and let's enjoy the journey. Amen.

dance

To dance is to be out of yourself. Larger, more beautiful, more powerful. This is power, it is glory on earth and it is yours for the taking. —Agnes de Mille

I don't miss the days before GPS, when I would end up at my surprise destination and wonder, *Where did I go wrong?*

There are followers of Christ asking the same question: Where did we go wrong? We tried our hardest to get where we thought we were supposed to go. We tried following all the instructions, but we still feel a sense of failure. Exhausted, disoriented, and lost, it's tempting to give up hope and lose faith.

How did we get off course? How do we find our way back?

Paul takes the believers of Galatia back to the beginning.

> *I would like to learn just one thing from you: Did you receive the Spirit by the works of the law, or by believing what you heard?* (Galatians 3:2)

Let's be real. **We all know we are saved by grace through faith. But we also know believers are notorious for handing each other to-do lists in the name of discipleship.** It sounds a little like this:

Put down that cigarette. God's temple is not an ashtray. We're supposed to be the aroma of life, not Marlboro. Besides, you'll need both hands to turn the pages during your quiet time. Here's a daily plan for finishing the Bible in a year, with little check-off boxes to mark your progress. And how often do you get paid? Good, write a check for 10 percent each pay period. And don't worry, if you forget to do any of this, your accountability partner will be all over you like a cheap suit... in love, of course.

Can you feel the restriction? The stiffness of marching boots? The forced change in behavior? This is not the way of the Spirit. Feeling like a failure is not the same as feeling sorrowful over sin. It's something deeper—indicative that I'm marching and not living through the fullness of God's Spirit. The Spirit is the fullness of life.

Don't get me wrong. I'm all for purity, generosity, and hunger for God's Word. But not when they are forced upon us from the outside and pursued in the power of the flesh. No, all good things come from the movement of the Spirit within us. Purity, generosity, and hunger for the Word are all longings of His Spirit within us, and this fruit ripens by season, not by force.

Lord, whisper to me the story of our meeting—the story of my salvation—when I received Your grace by Your Spirit and believed what I had heard. Show me, right now, where I am still following the external rules of man-made religion by force, rather than following the internal GPS of Your Spirit. I choose trusting Your transformation over working it out on my own. Amen.

DAY 59

So what does a good teacher do? Create tension—but just the right amount.
—Donald Norman

Tension results from unknowns. It exists to keep an audience engaged and asking good questions. Tension evokes emotional investment and sets the stakes: Who is going to lose what, and how am I going to feel if it's lost?

In Galatians, Paul does a major job of heightening the tension between the law and grace. He builds the tension to the place where we have to face clear distinctions, and we have to choose between the two:

> *Did you receive the Spirit by the works of the law, or by believing what you heard?* (Galatians 3:2)

> *So again I ask, does God give you his Spirit and work miracles among you by the works of the law, or by your believing what you heard?* (Galatians 3:5)

We do a little dance because we know the answer, don't we? Spirit and belief, baby!

> *For if the inheritance depends on the law, then it no longer depends on the promise; but God in his grace gave it to Abraham through a promise.* **Why, then, was the law given at all?** (Galatians 3:18-19a, emphasis mine)

And our dance floor is suddenly still. Why *did* God give the law? If we don't need it, did God make a mistake?

What's at stake in Paul's question? Do we leave the entire Old Testament behind? What about the Ten Commandments? What about other rules in Scripture? Sure, we all want to answer "grace and belief," but don't we feel the tension with the law and rules too? What's at stake? Just about everything, including our inheritance—our freedom in Christ.

May the tension in Paul's question dismantle the shackles that keep you from dancing!

Thank You for incredible teachers such as Paul, who build tension so I might realize what's at stake if I add to Your grace. Give me understanding as to why I'm leaving legalism behind, so I will never be tempted to return, and so I can answer with grace and truth to others who need to be set free. Amen.

dance

It may be true that the law cannot make a man love me, but it can stop him from lynching me, and I think that's pretty important. —Martin Luther King Jr.

Before you rip out the pages of Deuteronomy and Leviticus, let's wrestle with the biblical tension between law and freedom. If the law can't save me, then why did God implement the law?

Let's start with what God did *not* intend for the law to accomplish, as put forth in Galatians:

- The law can't give you the Spirit of God. (3:2)
- The law can't mature you in your faith. (3:3)
- The law can't work miracles among you. (3:5)
- The law can't make you righteous. (3.6)
- The law can't justify you. (3:11)

So why did He give the law at all?

> *It was added because of transgressions until the Seed... had come.*
> (Galatians 3:19)

Let that sink in. God gave the law because of our depravity—our deep-rooted inclination, before we were in Christ, to sin against the standard of God's perfection. God added the law for a limited time while we were still in Adam.

Wait a second! How do we know it was for a limited time only? Look at the verse above once more:

*It was **added** because of transgressions **until** the Seed... had come.*

The law was confined by the limitations of time. It expired when the promised Seed of Abraham arrived. Abraham's covenant has no expiration date. But the law? It expired with Jesus!

This tension would be a great mystery if Paul hadn't solved it for us. Why did God implement the law? There are many reasons, and we will explore them over the next couple of days. But for now, realize that **the law came because of mankind's sinfulness and for a limited amount of time in the past so we can be free to dance with Jesus today.**

My eyes are opened to Your Sovereignty. May Your Spirit slow me down this week as I consider the weight of what it means to benefit from a plan of redemption that took thousands of years to unfold. I praise You that Your plans unfold throughout generations and centuries. Thank You for containing Your law by time, for the sake of preparation, as the time ripened for the coming of Your Son. Amen.

DAY 61

dance

We make a big mistake when we conclude that the law is the answer to bad behavior. In fact, the law alone stirs up more of such behavior. People get worse, not better, when you lay down the law. —Tullian Tchividjian

Some scholars suggest the law is "provocative." It not only names our sins, but also causes sin to increase. I agree.

When I was a little boy, we lived in the countryside of England. One day, as my friend and I were playing in the yard, my dad came outside and said, "Pete and Andy, come here!" We ran over. "Do NOT go over the wall at the end of the yard."

Andy and I had never even noticed the wall at the end of the yard until that moment—the moment it was forbidden. As soon as my dad left, we launched ourselves over the wall to the other side.

As we were frolicking in our disobedience, we heard a terrible grunt. I looked at Andy, "Was that you?" Andy shook his head.

We turned around to see a new addition to the neighborhood—a perturbed bull. We launched ourselves back over the wall only to find something more terrifying on the other side—my father.

> *The law was brought in so that the trespass might increase.*
> (Romans 5:20)

Listen, I'd never wanted to cross that wall until Dad told me I couldn't. Then I wanted nothing more than to disobey (not realizing there was something harmful on the other side of disobedience).

The law operates in just that manner. **God gave the law because of the sinfulness of mankind.** *But it was never intended to put a stop to sinfulness.* **In fact, according to Romans it actually** *caused us to sin even more.*

Was the law flawed? No. The problem wasn't in the law—God's perfect standard for humanity. The problem is in us; the problem is the "power of sin." (See Romans 7.)

In His sovereignty, God allowed us to sin to a point of desperation—to a place where our souls cry out for our need for a Savior. The law works when it points us to Jesus! Have you gotten to that point? Are you there now?

God Who Sees, I thank You for calling right, right and wrong, wrong. Today, I make no more excuses for my sin. Today, I stop giving it fanciful names that make sin sound nicer and tamer than what it is. I praise You for using the law to show me my need for Your mercy. I thank You for the covering of grace. I pray Your indwelling Spirit suffocates the desires of the power of sin today so I can dance the hours away. Amen.

To be sure, the Spirit does use both God's law and God's gospel in our sanctification. But the law and the gospel do very different things.
—Tullian Tchividjian

The law is not designed to make you a disciple. The law is designed to make you desperate.

As sin increased and darkness flourished, the law came and called sin by its name. No longer could someone commit adultery without realizing God had pronounced it wrong. No longer could one neighbor steal from another and make excuses before the Lord. Sin increased, sin was called sin, and people were living in sin and dying in sin and being controlled by sin.

It was a time of desperation! A season of honest transparency when the created cried out to Creator, "Is there more to life than this? This feels like death!"

The law cannot do what Christ did. The law can't impart *life*.

> *The law was brought in so that the trespass might increase. But where sin increased, grace increased all the more.* (Romans 5:20)

Where earthbound sin and heavenly grace collide, we find a storm of epic proportions—and that's where we encounter the full strength of God's love. It is here that we understand why the skies darkened and the sun disappeared in the hours of Jesus' death. We can see how the temple's veil— with the thickness of a man's hand—could be torn in two by the raging of God's grace.

The law was not designed to make you a disciple; it was designed to make you desperate. Its burden of perfection enslaves. The desire to sin overwhelms. The justice we deserve is more than we can bear. As prisoners, we cry out for undeserved freedom, for we know we are guilty.

And in that moment—when you admit you can't live the life you deserve—you are met by an overwhelming storm of God's grace.

It is in your desperation that He saves you. It is out of darkness that He disciples you.

And it is in this grace that you find life.

Lord, without You, I'm unworthy of You. At my worst I hear you whisper I am loved. The moment I realize I have nothing to give, You remind me You've given me everything in Jesus. Your grace is a storm that washes me clean of my sin. I surrender to that storm today. I rest in the cool waters of Your forgiveness. Through Your Spirit, may I live a life worthy of all You've done. Amen.

dance

Let us be eager to leave what is familiar for what is true. —Francis Chan

The law was not designed to bring freedom. It was designed as a fence creating a place of captivity and protection for God's people. Paul knew the first step to dancing was to stop marching. Marching is a sign of imprisonment; it's a sign of living under the law.

> Before the coming of this faith, we were held in custody under the law, locked up until the faith that was to come would be revealed… Now that this faith has come, we are no longer under a guardian.
> (Galatians 3:23, 25)

During Paul's day, wealthy families hired a *pedagogos* to care for their sons between the ages of 6 and 18. These "guardians" were responsible for all of the child's training and often held brutal discipline in high regard. Yet they also played an important role in protecting these sons from the unwanted public advances common in Roman times.

That's the image of a guardian that Paul has in his mind as he writes about our freedom from the law—a strict guardian that both disciplined and protected. Yes, those images still appear in many forms in our world today, "guardians" that seem so familiar and so safe… but are they?

> So in Christ Jesus [we] are all children of God through faith…
> (Galatians 3:26)

Now that we are saved, we are free to be defined by Christ and nothing else. He invites us to a place of full dependency upon Him, and in this place we are everything. But the choice is ours, moment by moment. Will we, indeed, eagerly leave what is familiar for what is true?

Lord Jesus, I eagerly confess that You are the way, the truth, and the life. I choose to live each day in radical trust that we are experiencing life together. I leave behind all titles given to me by this world and embrace the one title that matters—a child of God. Beneath the stricture of the law, I saw clearly the beauty of Your gentle grace. This freedom—this intimacy—is what You had in mind since creation. May we walk in this place together, may we dance in this place together today. Amen.

I have not failed. I've just found 10,000 ways that won't work.
—Thomas A. Edison

You'd think sincere and pure devotion to Christ would be one of the qualifiers God looks for in a person He calls to pastor. You'd think. Paul writes,

> *I am afraid that just as Eve was deceived by the serpent's cunning, your minds may somehow be led astray from your sincere and pure devotion to Christ.* (2 Corinthians 11:3)

I was already a pastor when the Lord gently showed me that this "sincere and pure devotion" was missing from my life. I'd read this verse dozens of times before; it wasn't new to me. However, for months I'd been acutely aware of my struggles, failures, and shortcomings. I was numb and needed help getting out of the funk.

When I read this verse at this particular time, clarity came. "Lord," I asked, "have I lost my sincere and pure devotion to You?"

"Pete," He replied, "you never had it."

God has great methods of alleviating the funk, doesn't He?

Turns out, my sense of failure was rooted in a wrong identity. I defined myself as pastor, elder, leader, husband, and father. I'd taken on a dozen different identities and was crumbling under the march when God created me to live out one primary identity: a son of God. **Think about that. There are 10,000 different roles on earth, but if you are in Christ, you are a child of God.** *Nothing else matters.*

Purity is a singleness of substance. One thing is not mixed with another. Paul knew this—that devotion is pure when undivided and uncontaminated. From this singular devotion, all other aspects of life, love, and relationship fall into proper perspective. But that perspective only comes when you see clearly who you already are as His child—that's where sincere and pure devotion comes naturally.

Lord, take me into a place of freedom as Your child. Uncover my primary identity. Through Your Spirit, empower me to take hold of that identity and make it the one thing—the point of origin—in which everything I do here on earth is rooted. Amen.

Don't ever discount the cry of your heart. God may be working in your heart to bring about his sovereign plan. —K. Howard Joslin

I was with my daughter at a retreat, when the speaker instructed us to write an honest prayer. I was in a bad place at this time, struggling in my own failures and flaws. My first thought was, *No way.* My second thought was, *I guess everyone else is doing it.* My third thought was, *I'd better do it too—you know, as a model for my daughter…*

In spite of my resistance, words started to flow. I wrote a raw and honest prayer—stuff from the guts of my heart and the bowels of my soul. I wrote feeling certain that no one else would ever have to read it or know the struggle that lurked beneath my whitewashed pastor image.

Sometimes I reread that prayer and remember what it was like to be honest with myself and with God. But I also read it aloud when I'm speaking at a retreat or even on a Sunday morning, and I always get the same response from the crowd—*knowing looks.* They get it. They've either been there or are there—stuck in a sense of failure in their relationship with God.

What would a truly honest prayer of yours sound like today?

Now, let me show you the passage that uproots the sense of defeat that likely lurks in your soul:

> *So in Christ Jesus you are all children of God through faith.*
> (Galatians 3:26)

We feel like failures when we don't understand our sonship, that we are His children. We feel like failures when our efforts to perform spiritually don't produce the results we wanted. What do we want? We want to experience intimacy with God. But guess what? Performance-based intimacy is not intimacy at all—it's legalism. We are no longer living by a pass-fail system, but by a system of faith in Jesus.

Because you have faith in Christ Jesus, you are a child of God. Nothing else matters. So pray honest prayers of defeat if that is where you are today. Pray to and struggle with your Father. May intimacy, strength, and confidence be the result.

Lord, Giver of Faith, sometimes my fears keep me from being honest with You. Remind me today of the truth that brings light to the darkest corners of my life—the truth that I am not Your child through great faith, or complete faith, or perfect faith. I am a child of God through faith. Pure, simple, no adjective included—faith. Amen.

God did not give the Bible so we could master him or it; God gave the Bible so we could live it, so we could be mastered by it. The moment we think we've mastered it, we have failed to be readers of the Bible. —Scot McKnight

The sacrament of baptism in some early churches would make us blush today. New followers of Christ would come to the water in their old robes, strip down to only their birthday suits, be dipped in the water, and, upon exiting, receive new white robes.

It is beautiful imagery that states, "I'm coming to Christ and leaving my old life—this old cloak—on the shore. I'm bringing nothing with me, as I have nothing of value to offer Him. I'm crucified with Christ, buried with Christ, and raised to new life with Christ. As I step into this new life, I am clothed with Christ. I am unified with Christ."

> *So in Christ Jesus you are all children of God through faith, for all of you who were baptized into Christ have clothed yourselves with Christ.* (Galatians 3:26-27)

The context for baptism in the early church is really interesting. The word *baptizo* comes from *bapto*, which means to "dip and dye." The idea was that a white cloth when dipped in the dye came up different. The cloth identified with the dye and was forever changed. (This was before the days of Clorox.)

What does it mean to be in Christ? It means He envelopes you, He clothes you, He identifies with you so strongly that you are inseparable from Christ— like the dye in the cloth. As His child, you are swallowed up into Christ. *No other identity matters.*

Yes, you are a child of God. *Nothing else matters.*

Jesus, I come to You with nothing of eternal value and stand before You bare, naked, and exposed. You see me for who I truly am and still extend Your hand in invitation. I accept this new life. I accept the clothing of Christ. I don't always know how to live it, but I identify with You and ask that You will give a profound awareness of how You have dipped and dyed me in You. Amen.

I know there's a place you walked, where love falls from the trees. My heart is like a broken cup. I only feel right on my knees. I spit out like a sewer hole, yet still receive your kiss. How can I measure up to anyone now, after such a love as this? Who are you? Who, who, who, who? —The Who

Soooo, who are *you*? You might answer:

I'm a man, a woman, a teenager. I'm a Republican, a Democrat, a Baptist, a Methodist. I'm a Millennial, a Gen X-er, a Baby Boomer. I'm Latino, African American, Caucasian, Asian. I'm well-off, I'm struggling, I'm making ends meet. I'm a father of two, a mom of five. I'm single. I'm married. I'm divorced. I'm separated.

Sure, some of those descriptions might be a fit. For years, I introduced myself as a pastor, a leader, a preacher, a radio guy. However, these were all *secondary* identities. It took the Lord to show me, "Pete, you're a son of God. Nothing else matters."

Even after becoming followers of Christ, we can continue to live out of our secondary identities. What are our secondary identities? Anything other than the truth about being a child of God.

Listen, the cross leveled the ground beneath it. There are no longer distinctions beyond the fact that we are *all* children of God through faith in Christ Jesus.

> *There is neither Jew nor Gentile, neither slave nor free, nor is there male and female, for you are all one in Christ Jesus.* (Galatians 3:28)

What's your *primary* identity? You are a child of God through faith in Jesus.

Paul goes on to say in Galatians 4:6 that your soul can cry out to God, *"Abba,* Father.*" Abba* is translated as "Daddy." That might seem trivial, but really think about everything this name implies! Children run to "Daddy." They ride on their "daddy's" shoulders. They tuck themselves under "Daddy's" arms. They tug on his hand—and they know their "daddy" is smitten with them.

Please, get this: **Today, you can call Him "Daddy" with all of the random, giddy, spontaneous passion of a child. Because you *are* His kid, and *nothing*—nothing—can keep you from His embrace today.**

Daddy, show me today how every single person on earth is either a slave or a son. May that realization change how I live. May it change how I love others. May it erase my sense of failure and charge me with a need to engage Your Spirit in me to follow You in reckless abandon and trust as You lead me in the dance today. Amen.

If you eat a balanced diet you get all the vitamins and minerals you need and you don't need any supplement and overdosing can actually be more harmful. —Subodh Gupta

People who are concerned about their health tend to be serious about vitamins. Many open their pack of supplements each morning, swallow down the pills, and then eat whatever they wish for the rest of the day. They take supplements to cover the inadequacy of their diet.

Then there are those who take supplements to supercharge their health. They swallow their horse-sized pills right before they eat their gluten-free, high-protein, low-fat, low-carb, sugar-free breakfast. Their supplements are back-up insurance. Through proper nutrition, they already have everything they need, but just in case…

Interesting, isn't it? Here's the point: The church in Galatia approached their faith this same way and so do many of us. They had Jesus, but they weren't sure He was enough. Teachers came along and told them, "Hey, Jesus is great, but you need a boost—a supplement—to the Gospel. You need to add some law to your faith diet." The Galatians, on a spiritual health kick, jumped on board. After all, the law had been good for them in the past; why not use it to supplement faith today?

When Paul realized what was happening, he didn't mince words.

> *"Evidently some people are throwing you into confusion and are trying to pervert the gospel of Christ."* (Galatians 1:7)

Bam! Paul hit this hard, and so should we. Jesus requires no supplement. His provision is complete. To add to the pure Gospel of God's amazing grace isn't just unnecessary, it changes the Good News and makes it no Gospel at all!

Think about that. It's that serious. It's that damaging to your spiritual health.

Lord, thank you that your grace requires no supplement whatsoever! Thank you for Paul's teaching that highlights what's at stake when I'm tempted to let legalism impact my spiritual health. I don't want to change the Good News, I want to embrace it and be free in it. Amen.

If a potato can produce vitamin C, why can't we? Within the animal kingdom only humans and guinea pigs are unable to synthesize vitamin C in their own bodies. Why us and guinea pigs? No point asking. Nobody knows.
—Bill Bryson

A lot of people make a lot of money telling others how to become godlier on their own. I call it the "muscle-up" strategy of spiritual growth. They write books that say we all have the ability to make ourselves more like God. Each chapter has a title that tells them where to start. **Yeah, if you're serious about Jesus, it's time to get in God's gym and start pumping some spiritual iron, right?**

These books offer supplements to the Bible; they pick up where the Bible left off.

Pick up where the Bible left off? Don't email me yet, but I hope alarms are sounding as you read, because these days aren't unlike the early days in Galatia. People are still stirring up trouble, selling the idea that believers need something more in their life with Christ. They say, "Jesus is a good starting place, but if you are going to grow, you need to do something extra."

Modern semantics have changed the wording a bit; we don't call it "law" anymore. Instead we label it with more acceptable names—like "disciplines." If you exercise spiritual disciplines, you grow. Exercising spiritual disciplines helps you produce godliness in your life, right?

Please hear me! I am not anti prayer, fasting, or Scripture reading. Those are all wonderful things if done in freedom by the leading and the power of God's Spirit. I disagree with the belief that self-disciplines can produce godliness. Only God can produce godliness.

> *He saved us, not because of righteous things we had done, but because of his mercy. He saved us through the washing of rebirth and renewal by the Holy Spirit.* (Titus 3:5)

This truth is music for the dance! *God* does the saving. *God* gives the mercy. *His Holy Spirit* washes, regenerates, and renews. We need not muscle-up, only trust in what God has already done and allow Him to be our strength today.

Father, transformation excites me. It's an adventure to look back and realize I'm not the same as when I started. Continue to renew my thinking, my priorities, and my love for others and Your creation. May I learn to rest in Your strength according to what You have already accomplished in me through Jesus. Amen.

dance

Have no fear of perfection—you'll never reach it. —Salvador Dali

God doesn't grade on the curve. You don't get a break because you think you are doing better than others, and a 99 percent on your review isn't going to get you promoted in God's Kingdom. **Listen, if you're going to try to prove yourself worthy according to the Bible, you'll need to keep all 613 commands because the law requires perfection.**

> *For whoever keeps the whole law and yet stumbles at just one point is guilty of breaking all of it.* (James 2:10)

How could a person keep the entire law? King David spoke of meditating on the law day and night, and he still committed adultery. The law consumed his thought life, but ultimately it revealed his inability to achieve perfection and his great need for God.

Not much has changed today. We are still unable to live beneath the law's demand for perfection, and we still have an incredible need for God.

> *Christ redeemed us from the curse of the law by becoming a curse for us...* (Galatians 3:13)

Please ponder this for just a moment, because it can change your whole day for the better: **Jesus desires for us to be free to live and free to be consumed by His perfect love. We can leave the curse of perfection behind.**

Do you get it? If you're like me, you probably need to "get it" every day. You don't have to worry about the law, and—even though we know sin is wretched—you don't have to fear when you stumble. Life in the Spirit is not performance based. You are not accepted or rejected based on your behavior. **The divine standard has been satisfied by the Divine sacrifice, and that changes everything!**

Perfect Father, I look up today and confess I've been running toward the wrong finish line. I've stumbled (and prayed no one is watching). I've failed (and feared that it made me a failure). Show me the way of acceptance so I might walk in it. Lead me away from this curse and into the gift of grace so I can be free to follow Your Holy Spirit, according to Your living Word today. Let's dance! Amen.

dance

It is perfectly true, as philosophers say, that life must be understood backwards. But they forget the other proposition, that it must be lived forwards. —Søren Kierkegaard

When I talk about law and grace, there are always those who say, "But Pete, the law is the foundation and grace is the building. The Old Testament is law; the New Testament is grace. Are we supposed to ignore the entire Old Testament?"

No way. The Old Testament is not just about law, and the New Testament is not the first introduction of grace.

Listen, this is important: The Old Testament is about grace and the New Testament is about grace. The Christ system—the faith system, the grace system—was in play way back with Abraham. That was 430 years before the law came to be. The law system was thrown into the middle of that.

> *In other words, it is not the children by physical descent who are God's children, but it is the children of the promise who are regarded as Abraham's offspring.* (Romans 9:8)

The promise and covenant between God and Abraham was first, and it was a covenant of faith. "Father Abraham" was declared righteous because He believed God's promises—and we are children of that promise! The promise to Abraham was not nullified by the law system, which was introduced later. The law was fulfilled in Jesus so that the promise stood alone once again.

Yes, Abraham looked ahead to Christ. We look back to Christ. It's always been about Jesus.

Father of Eternity, I have a finite mind with my experiences limited to this tiny point on the timeline of history. So I'm pretty amazed when I look back and realize the extent to which You've orchestrated grace. It's beautiful. Your grace calls to me from all pages of Scripture and creates a stereo of sound that invites me to dance in worship. Today I thank You for the promise of yesterday, the grace of today, and the hope of tomorrow. Amen.

dance

I used to get really ticked about preachers who talked too much about grace, because they tempted me to not be disciplined. I figured what people needed was a kick in the butt… I believed that if word got out about grace, the whole church was going to turn into a brothel. I was a real jerk, I think.
—Donald Miller

Is there anything wrong with reading your Bible every day? Of course not.

Is there anything wrong with wanting to pray every day? Of course not.

But here's what some of us do: We come up with a contract—a plan of action that we think will make us better Christians and produce fruits of godliness in our lives. Then we get pretty proud of ourselves when we stick to the contract. We start to compare ourselves to others and feel better because we are "godlier," since our faith is being supplemented by so many spiritual exercises.

It's a workout. But is it working out?

Then there are those of us who have made up a contract and realize that everyone else in the world could probably keep this contract except us. So we suck it up, make a new spiritual New Year's resolution, and try again (or just finally give it up because, deep down, we know we stink at contracts). So each morning we count up the number of failures from the day before, and pretty soon we feel like the bottom turd in the manure pile of spiritual immaturity.

Whether we're proud of ourselves or beating ourselves up doesn't matter. **Contracts with ourselves never end well. The end is either self-righteousness or self-condemnation. The same thing is missing from both scenarios— Jesus—faith, trust, and intimacy with Jesus who alone can lead us in the dance.**

By saying we need to supplement our faith with works and contracts, what we are really saying is that Jesus isn't enough.

> *"I am the bread of life. Whoever comes to me will never go hungry, and whoever believes in me will never be thirsty."* (John 6:35)

Jesus is enough. He becomes more than we could ever imagine when we say no to contracts and walk with Him by faith moment by moment, song by song.

Jesus, I know You are enough. I have this memorized but not internalized. I desire more—more intimacy, more adventure—but rather than turning to You, I fill up with the latest spiritual workout. I'm shredding the contract—whatever deal I've made with myself, I'm ripping it up. It's just You and me. And that's exactly enough. Now… lead me, please… Amen.

People who LIKE movies have a favorite. People who LOVE movies couldn't possibly choose. —Nicole Yatsonsky

My kids used to come up and ask me, "Dad, who's your favorite?" I would answer the same way every time: "You're all my favorite." They would walk away disappointed. I said *all*, but it kind of sounded like *none*. Now, if we don't know the truth, we might feel the same when God says,

> *So in Christ Jesus you are all children of God…* (Galatians 3:26)

Then one day, one of my sons asked my wife, "Mommy, who's your favorite kid?" She grabbed him by the shoulders, looked him in the eyes, and said, "Liam, *you* are my favorite child."

He got this huge smile on his face. "Really? Yes!" He was so happy.

My daughter had overheard the conversation. A little while later, she asked, "Mom, who is your favorite child?"

Once again, my wife grabbed my daughter by the shoulders, looked her in the eyes, and said, "Annika, *you* are my favorite child."

Our third child overheard that conversation and, as you can imagine, he came in and asked the same question. My wife responded in the same way, "Cameron, *you* are my favorite."

She and I said the same thing, didn't we? "You're all my favorite." But it felt different when she said it. It felt *personal* as they each—individually—realized *they* were her favorite.

I'm going to make a wild statement here: *You* are God's favorite. Stop and feel this. **God's capacity to love is infinitely more extravagant than any earthly parent, and He's grabbing *you* by the shoulders and looking *you* in the eyes right now, saying, "You, *you* are my favorite!"**

Lord, man and woman, boy and girl, we are unable to express the full thanks we feel at being Your children. Your child. If I'm honest, I can't completely imagine actually being Your favorite. It blows my mind. I pray Your Holy Spirit will help me understand just how much You love me. Amen.

dance

No one is born hating another person because of the color of his skin, or his background, or his religion. People must learn to hate, and if they can learn to hate, they can be taught to love, for love comes more naturally to the human heart than its opposite. —Nelson Mandela

I had a friend in college who grew up in a small Southern town. The elders at his church—every single one—were members of the Klu Klux Klan. The two largest deacons had a very simple job—they were the church bouncers. If a black man tried to get in, they would turn him away.

Can't you hear the Spirit whispering in the background of that church, "But that man… *he* is My favorite. Let My favorite one in!"

There can be no favoritism in the body of Jesus—and yet there is. Race, economic status, and gender have *all* been areas of favoritism in the church for years. **The good news, my friends, is that we have a choice. We can choose to see** *only* **favorites. And we can choose to reject favoritism.**

People often ask me to pray for them. And I do; it's a privilege. But I'm quick to correct the idea that God pays more attention to the prayers of a pastor, or that I have some sort of "yes" card to pull with the Lord. Now, of course I know that *I'm* His favorite, but I also know *you* are His favorite too. **Because we are all His favorites; there is no favoritism in the family of God.**

Favoritism says that, for some inappropriate reason, some people are treated better than others, some receive superior opportunities than others, and some get more blessing than others. Paul destroyed that lie and, by the power of the Spirit, you can begin to live the truth!

> *There is neither Jew nor Gentile, neither slave nor free, nor is there male and female, for you are all one in Christ Jesus.* (Galatians 3:28)

Father, we are all Your favorites. Let sibling rivalry and competition be gone in Your family. Let there be hospitality and selflessness and high esteem of each other. Let me, imperfect me, love them with Your perfect love. Yes, teach me the language of Your love. Amen.

If you want to do the work of God, pay attention to people. Notice them. Especially the people nobody else notices. —John Ortberg

Have you ever heard a prayer that sounded more like a punch? Imagine this: Every morning, many Orthodox Jewish men would pray a prayer that went like this: "Bless me, God, that He did not make me a Gentile. Bless me, God, that He did not make me ignorant or a slave. Bless me, God, that He did not make me a woman."

Ouch. Three punches in a row: Racism. Elitism. Sexism.

Although Paul was probably raised on that prayer, he radically broke rank and wrote a new proclamation that conveyed the social dynamics of God's new Kingdom and His desire for the new body of Christ. It went like this:

> *There is neither Jew nor Gentile, neither slave nor free, nor is there male and female, for you are all one in Christ Jesus.* (Galatians 3:28)

It's a stunning reversal of the Jewish prayer, revealing a practical transformation in the way we can see:

- "You thank God you're not a Gentile?" No! In Christ there's no longer Jew nor Gentile.

- "You thank God you're not a slave?" Not anymore! In Christ there is neither slave nor free.

- "You thank God you're not a woman?" Forget it! In Christ there are only co-heirs of the promise—for we are all one in Christ Jesus.

These are radical statements, friends. Which leads us back to an extraordinary element of the Gospel: *Each of us is His favorite, so there can be no favoritism!*

Jesus wants to change the way we see people—the way *you* see people. Are you willing to let Him give you new eyes today?

God Who Sees, I have imperfect vision and can often be caught looking at myself. I pray today for healing in the area of favoritism. Uproot this from my life. Give me Your eyes to see the way You see, so I can notice people that no one else notices. Please, reveal one person in need today, then speak to me about how to love that person. Amen.

dance

When someone you love makes compassion, kindness, forgiveness, respect and God an option, you can be sure they have made you an option, as well.
—Shannon L. Alder

Favoritism creates disposable humans. We see it in every war, in the Holocaust, in the Middle East, and in our own neighborhoods. In Jesus' day, women were among the discarded… literally.

In his book *Who Is This Man?*, John Ortberg shares that the Roman world averaged 140 men for every 100 women. You see, the Law of Romulus in Rome required a father to raise all his healthy sons and only the first healthy daughter. After that, daughters were disposable without legal consequence. In one Roman city, Delphi, only 1 out of 600 known families chose to raise more than one daughter. Can you imagine?

Josephus, a famous Jewish historian, wrote, "The woman, says the law, is inferior to the man." Thus, because men were favored, women became disposable.

Jesus went out of his way to invite the discarded and rejected into the Kingdom. He was radical in this way—inviting outsiders to become insiders.

Think about the woman at the well in John 4. Her ethnicity is considered inferior, her gender is considered inferior, and she had been abandoned—either through death or divorce—by five men. She's despised, discarded, and rejected. So when Jesus speaks to her, she's shocked. I love how Jesus responded to her shock. *If you knew Me…* (para. 4:10).

- *If you knew Me,* then you'd know I don't have favorites.

- *If you knew Me,* then you'd know I accept you and love you just as you are.

- *If you knew Me,* then you'd know you are priceless to Me—I will give all of Myself to redeem you.

Scripture says that when the disciples returned, they marveled that Jesus was talking to a woman. **Listen, when we start to see others as Jesus sees them—as all His favorites—our behavior can be just as radical.** We *will* find ourselves engaged in conversations that blow our minds, blow their minds, and blow the minds of those watching. Jesus is radically accepting, and He is in you! When you know that about Him, He will love this way through you.

Lord, my prayer today is simple. I want to know You more. I want to know the depths of Your compassion, the extent of Your kindness, the freedom of Your forgiveness, the regard for Your Creation, and the place of belonging found in Your love. Then love the rejected ones through me. Amen.

When we see people that are impoverished and people who are dealt an unfair hand, then if we have the power to help them, we should try to do that.
—John Legend

One sister is working her tail off in the kitchen, while the other is curled up at the feet of Jesus, in a room full of men, listening to the rabbi teach. The sister who is hot and overwhelmed in the kitchen complains to the rabbi, but the rabbi says,

> *"You are worried and upset about many things, but few things are needed—or indeed only one. Mary has chosen what is better, and it will not be taken away from her."* (Luke 10:41-42)

And today, we read it and think, *It's better to go to church than it is to cook breakfast.*

But think about it. Really. **Until Jesus, that sitting sister never had the choice.** Sitting at the feet of a rabbi to be taught was not even allowed unless you were male. Jesus initiated the opportunity for women to become disciples, and it was a *radical move.*

> *There is neither Jew nor Gentile, slave nor free, nor is there male and female, for you are all one in Christ Jesus.* (Galatians 3:28)

Where are you on that list? I'm not of Jewish descent, so I would have been a Gentile. What about you? Are you someone who struggles on minimum wage, or are you free to make financial decisions at your leisure? Are you male or are you female?

The truth is that we are disciples of Christ only because Jesus confronted favoritism and invited all to sit at His feet. Why would He do this? Because Jesus knows that our highest calling is never found in categorical labels. Our highest calling is found in Christ.

No more favoritism in the body of Christ. Only invitation. There is plenty of room at His feet. And if you really need breakfast—this is America, they have donuts at church while you learn about the rabbi.

Jesus, I don't fully understand the radical change You brought into the world. What I do see is magnetic. It's brave and bold and necessary. It makes me realize I'm part of a Kingdom that holds freedom within its boundaries—a freedom for all. Give me a hunger for Your Word, an appetite for study and understanding. Knowing You set people free; knowing You will set people free. Amen.

Love and pregnancy and riding on a camel cannot be hid. —Arabic Proverb

I have a friend on Facebook who documented her entire pregnancy by standing in front of a large chalkboard. If I click through her album, I can watch her flat tummy begin to protrude, covering a little more of that chalkboard every week. Sure, a number on the board tells me how long she's been pregnant, but the side profile is all about how much she's showing.

But I have a question: Is *she* really showing? I don't think so. I think *the baby is showing himself* from inside her.

That baby's growth represents new life and that new life shows naturally.

Here's the point: Our life in Christ is like a pregnancy. It really is. The Spirit of Jesus is in us. The more we let Him live through us, the more Christ shows in our love and our actions. In fact, Paul even uses the metaphor of pregnancy in his letter to the Galatians:

> *My dear children, for whom I am again in the pains of childbirth until Christ is formed in you…* (4:19)

Until Christ is formed in you…

The word "formed" in this verse is *morpho*, a Greek medical term used, in places, to describe fetal development.

Wow, what a beautiful picture of surrender to "Christ in us"! **So I'm thinking that for men and women alike, Christian living is all about being pregnant with new life and letting that new life show.** How is your side profile? Are you letting Him show?

Famous One, I admit that I live in a society of self-promotion, and I tend to show self more often than I let You show. I ask Your Holy Spirit to shift my desire and shift my dependence. I'm done trying to show You on my own. May my life become more about You and less about me today! I belong to You. You are in me. Show Yourself as You choose today. Amen.

dance

When you do things from your soul, you feel a river moving in you, a joy.
—Rumi

Every once in a while, when someone decides to get honest, I hear some real, raw questions: "Why do I feel like I'm faking this Christian life? **I was happy when I got saved, but I've lost my joy.** What am I doing wrong?"

Hey, if you feel that way, I don't think you're doing anything wrong. Life with Christ is all about showing—not *us* showing off, but letting *Jesus* show from within us. Paul likened it to a pregnancy.

Most pregnancies start out with real joy. *New life is growing.* Sure, someone might vomit. Clothes don't fit, skin gets stretched. Then there's the day you can't see your toes. You know they are there because you can wiggle them—but see them or touch them? Forget it.

Lost joy is sort of the same. Joy is still there. It's a product of the Spirit who lives in you. But sometimes your concerns obstruct the life of the Spirit. And you're left wondering, *Didn't I used to have joy?*

The ebb and flow of joy that you've experienced—it happened to the early church in Galatia too. Paul writes to them,

> *Where, then, is your blessing of me now?* (Galatians 4:15)

Joy was there. But something shifted. This group of people who once went out of their way to care for him now treated Paul as an enemy. This church that once danced in the joy of freedom now lived beneath the burden of legalism.

So how can you *be* joyful again?

Well, there is only one thing to do when you can't see your toes—wiggle them and make sure they're still around. Thus, there's one thing you can do when you can't feel your joy: Let your Jesus show.

Let Him live through you again. Reach up to Him with empty hands and an open mind. Tell Him you are willing to let Him show through you. Open your hands in generosity, invite someone over for dinner, reach out at church even if you feel you don't fit. Anticipate Jesus as He shows Himself to others through you. **It won't take long to realize your joy is still living in you— because He is that joy!**

Lord, sometimes my own worries and concern distract me from the truth that Your Spirit is in me. However, just because I can't see You doesn't mean You aren't there. Let Your love flow from me like a current so I might have ever-present joy. I'm listening; I'm watching; I'm ready to let You show Yourself to someone in need today. Amen.

dance

I usually claim that pregnant women should not read books about pregnancy and birth. Their time is too precious. They should, rather, watch the moon and sing to the baby in the womb. —Michel Odent

When it comes to pregnancy and Christianity, everyone has advice. Lots of advice. And for some reason, they feel free to tell you all they think they know—whether you ask for it or not. While they might have good intentions, it feels like they are draining your joy and enslaving you to rules.

If you're pregnant, it goes down like this: Don't eat sushi. Don't drink caffeine. Avoid hotdogs, raw meat, and exercise. But don't *not* exercise. Sleep on your side with six pillows. Find a birthing center with a midwife. Reject the epidural. Embrace the pain. Reject the formula. Embrace the cloth diapers, etc., etc., etc., etc., etc.

If you are in Christ, legalism can feel a lot like that. The Christian life isn't lived alone. We live our life with Christ alongside other believers, and some of those believers have plenty of advice on how to live for Christ.

You can be walking with Christ and doing what comes naturally between you and the Spirit. You are filled with Christ. You are growing and He's showing. You are overjoyed at the changes in your life. It's more about Him and less about you. And if the two of you could just continue like this until your earthly life was over— well, that would be all joy. But you can be building intimacy with God and learning to let Jesus show when someone comes in and tells you you're doing it all wrong.

This went down in Galatia. **False teachers came in and told the Galatians they were living life with Christ incompletely.** They gave the Galatians a list of rules to go along with that new life in Christ. **And somehow, the Galatians became star-crossed by these false teachers.** Paul calls these false teachers out.

> *Those people are zealous to win you over, but for no good. What they want is to alienate you from us, so that you may have zeal for them.*
> (Galatians 4:17)

What happens when we follow the critics' advice? When we start to believe that it's Jesus + Something? We are alienated from the true Gospel: Jesus + Nothing = Everything. And the minute that happens, true joy goes out the window.

Don't waste a day on any other gospel, for only one births joy.

God, I pray You give me a discerning ear that mutes false gospels, so I can seek only You and show only You. Please, reveal right now where I have let the advice and expectations of others rob me of joy. Let's go back to just me and You living through me today. Amen.

dance

If you love deeply, you're going to get hurt badly. But it's still worth it.
—C. S. Lewis

A number of years ago, I was standing in the church foyer when I noticed a woman whose tummy was swollen. She held the small of her back and walked slowly—gingerly. I went over, introduced myself, and asked, "When's the baby due?"

Silence…

You only make that mistake once.

Generally speaking you *can* usually tell when a person is pregnant. And that person is always female, which seems to be an unnecessary statement until you read how Paul describes himself to the Galatians:

> *My dear children, for whom I am again in the pains of childbirth until Christ is formed in you…* (4:19)

He is telling the Galatians that he has labored for them as a woman for a child. Not only once—when he shared the Gospel with them the first time—but twice, as he anxiously awaits their rejection of false teachers.

And then he tells the Galatians that he will not labor as though in birth only twice, but continuously *until Christ is formed in them.*

Essentially Paul says, "I will labor for you until you are the ones swollen by the fullness of Christ in you."

It's a hand-off of the pregnancy baton.

Paul's heart here is beautifully contrasted with the false teachers'. **The goal of the false teachers was to create followers of their own in Galatia.** They labored for their own gain. **But Paul—Paul was laboring with intense emotion until the day the Galatians were once again focused on Christ.** Paul would be pained until the full image of Christ showed in the Galatians like a baby shows in a pregnant woman.

Do you love anyone so deeply that their mistaken view of God pains you to the point of birthing pains?

Father, Paul loved with Your heart and saw people as You saw them. As a result, he was in agony when Your children missed the opportunity to have Christ form fully within them. I ask today that I may feel that same degree of pain. And Lord, I turn this over to You and ask that You would labor intensely through me for the salvation of those around me. Amen.

dance

I think that carrying a baby inside you is like running as fast as you can. It feels like finally letting go and filling yourself up to the wildest limits.
—Author Unknown

Christ is forming in us—taking shape and filling us in the same way a child fills his mother. We can even think of baptism as a pregnancy announcement. What you're saying when you get baptized is, "I'm pregnant! Jesus is in me."

And He is. He's starting to grow and change the way we look and how we relate to people.

> *My dear children, for whom I am again in the pains of childbirth until Christ is formed in you…* (Galatians 4:19)

Jesus *will* begin to show in our lives and the results are amazing. Listen to some stories I've encountered of Jesus showing, just in my part of the world.

- I knew a guy who was offered a tremendous promotion but it would have required an uprooting of his family. His kids were doing great in school, and his wife had a sense of purpose in the community. So he looked at his family and chose to turn down his promotion. *His Jesus was showing.*

- There's a businessman in our church who is a partner in a firm with other believers. At the end of the year, the partners gather together and agree upon a certain percentage of company profits to give to charity. Every time they write that check, *their Jesus is showing.*

- I know a woman whose joy is to meet over coffee with younger women and just listen and encourage them in their lives. She does this every day. Her schedule is full of coffee and lunch dates, birthdays and milestone reminders as she watches these young women flourish in life, singleness, marriage, first children, first jobs, discovery of purpose, and intimacy with God. When she's listening and encouraging, *her Jesus is showing.*

So next time you see someone do something that has evidence of God all over it, let the person know. It's like walking up to someone, putting your hand on his or her tummy, and saying, "Hey! Your Jesus is showing."

Jesus, I look at others around me and feel like their Jesus is showing more than mine. In fact, sometimes I feel so barren compared to others. Yet, I believe Your Spirit fills me. I rest in You and trust in You to live through me as You wish. And today, show me one way You want to encourage one person who is letting You show through his or her life. Amen.

dance

When you're drowning you don't think, I would be incredibly pleased if someone would notice I'm drowning and come and rescue me. *You just scream.* —John Lennon

I was swimming one morning and noticed another gentleman working with a swim instructor. She was using a noodle under his arms to practice the backstroke. After a while, she took the noodle away. With the floaties gone, he flailed. Water sprayed as his arms pounded against the surface of the pool. The instructor offered him the noodle—and then took it away again. More flailing. This went on for 20 minutes.

He was in the locker room when I left, so I decided to go over and ask if he wanted a tip. He seemed grateful, so I continued, "Just do this one thing: hold your breath. Your lungs will become like two big floaties."

"Thanks, man," he said. "Maybe I will sink less."

Does this sound like your life in Christ at all? **I've talked with countless people who feel like their Christian life is a repetitive cycle of sinking. Most feel like they are trying so hard and yet are still drowning.** *Drowning beneath the rules of Christian culture. Drowning beneath a need to please God.*

Many are screaming for someone to throw them a lifeline—just **one thing** that will keep them afloat, one thing to help them find their stroke so they can swim.

Good news, friends. Paul throws us a line—that one thing by which we can live—and I think it will help us all sink less.

> For in Christ Jesus neither circumcision nor uncircumcision has any value. The only thing that counts is faith expressing itself through love. (Galatians 5:6)

One thing counts. Just one thing. And guess what? It isn't what you wear or don't wear. It isn't what you watch or don't watch. It isn't what you own or don't own. This one thing is all about living. **If you feel like you're drowning, take a deep breath and focus on one thing: faith expressing itself through love today.**

Father, I'm grateful that You can count the number of hairs on our heads, the stars in the sky, the grains of sand on the shore. But You made me limited in ability, and I just need one thing to hold on to to keep from sinking. Thank You for the gift of faith. Thank You for expressing love toward me. Today, show me one person who needs that love... and by faith, express Your love through me. Amen.

dance

Always remember, your focus determines your reality. —George Lucas

In Christian living, I believe there are two directions of focus:

> You can either focus on the *law*, or you can focus on *grace*.
> You either focus on *performance*, or you focus on *freedom*.
> You either focus on *you*, or you focus on *Jesus*.

There is no in between.

> *Again I declare to every man who lets himself be circumcised that he is obligated to obey the whole law.* (Galatians 5:3)

Do you see what Paul is saying? Once you bend to one rule, you are obliged to keep them all. And in the case of historic Judaism—the root of the law—this would be a list of 613 points of law that you must obey *every day*.

Maybe you aren't all about the 613, but you are devoutly devoted to the Big Ten Commandments. Listen carefully, you can't bend to one point of legalism—not for even one point—**one unshakable adherence to the law obligates you to the law in its entirety.**

Paul lays out the consequences of choosing to focus on law over grace. If you choose even one point of obligation to the law, then:

* Christ is no longer of value to you.
* You are obliged to the entire law—every day, every rule.
* You have alienated yourself from Christ and fallen away from grace.

Get this: God has given you freedom. His grace flows to you freely like water from a garden hose. You can put a kink in the hose, if you desire, but His grace still flows toward you. Don't obsess over the rules but rejoice in your freedom.

It is for freedom that you have been set free. The rest—the honoring of God and esteeming of others—will flow naturally from that love of God that dwells in you.

So choose today what your focus will be. Either you are fixated on the freedom that lies before you, or you are fixated on the slavery that was left behind you. Only one can be your reality, so which do you choose?

God, here I stand in this freedom You gave me, and I'm tempted to look over my shoulder at the days of defined rules and regulations. Sometimes freedom intimidates me because I don't know what to do with it. So Lord, I release everything to You now. I'm ready to freely follow Your lead, ready to let You live Your life through me. Today, show me the steps to living out this one thing: this faith expressed through love. Amen.

Ballet dancers learn to perform pirouettes by a technique called "spotting"—focusing on just one thing. This singular focus minimizes movement of inner ear fluid, thus decreasing dizziness and increasing balance. —BBC News

There are enough rules and restrictions in the Old Testament law to make your head spin—613, to be exact. Most of us don't have a clue what those 613 rules are, but we know the summary. We've got The Ten—the Ten Commandments.

Still, the 10 are nothing without the other 603. If you follow the law, you must follow it to the letter. **So what, exactly, are we supposed to focus on? Can we narrow these commands down to one?** A young lawyer—a Jewish student of the law—asked Jesus this very question.

> *"Teacher, which is the greatest commandment in the Law?" Jesus replied: "'Love the Lord your God with all your heart and with all your soul and with all your mind.' This is the first and greatest commandment. And the second is like it: 'Love your neighbor as yourself.' All the Law and the Prophets hang on these two commandments."* (Matthew 22:36-40)

What's the greatest commandment? Can you reduce the hundreds to just one thing? Yeah, you really can. Forget the 613 rules in the Old Testament. Forget the expectations and obligations the world and the Church place on you. **You can focus, just focus on the greatest command that everything else hangs on: Love.**

So if the Christian life is a dance—and I believe it is—then all good dancers know that before they can turn, they must determine their point of spotting. Before we can effectively show love to others, before we can honor relationships and commitments, before we can effectively stand firm in the spin cycle of life—we must determine that Jesus is our point of focus.

He is our faith. And when that faith is focused on Christ, the expression of love flows naturally and freely because He is the One and He is the Only, for God is love.

Can you feel the simplicity, the purity, and the power of that? Suddenly, the greatest command no longer feels like a command. It's something infinitely more powerful and profound than that. It is an overflow of the Love that dwells in us.

Lord of the Dance, I won't take my eyes off You. Lead me in this dance. As my eyes are fixed upon You, whether I turn to the right or the left, let my hands open in love and generosity to others. I place a mustard seed of faith in You today. I ask that You would express that faith through me with love today. Show me who, show me how. Amen.

dance

The one thing we can never get enough of is love. And the one thing we never give enough of is love. —Henry Miller

So we have the one thing—the key—to the Christian life: *Faith expressing itself through love.*

Now, what does it mean?

- The word *faith* means trusting. Trusting in the finished work of Christ. Trusting that the cross was enough. Trusting Jesus is who He says He is and then depending on Him.

- The phrase *expressing itself* literally means working. Watch how the same Greek word is used in Ephesians 3:20, *"Now to him who is able to do immeasurably more than all we ask or imagine, according to his power that is at work within us…"*

The Greek word is *energeo.* You can see what English word comes from that. So the next time you are lacking some *energeo*, leave the coffee on the counter and grab some Holy Spirit. I hear He's a real pick-me-up.

In all seriousness, let's put it all together: **The Spirit is at work in us. As we trust in Him, He brings about active love—love that is full of life and full of energy. This active love is the dance.** It's the end of marching of performing and trying to please. It's the beginning of a life defined by freedom and rooted in love.

Faith expressing itself through love…

If Paul wanted you to take notes, he might say something like, "Trust Jesus and let love happen."

Trust Jesus and let love happen.

Can you imagine what our churches—all 325,000 North American churches—would be like if we all figured out how to trust Jesus and let love happen? What about our marriages? Or our friendships? Or our fear of the future?

Trust Jesus and let love happen. It's that one step that makes the Christian life a dance.

Jesus, work in me, work through me. I can hardly contain the excitement I feel knowing that Your active love is an endless supply. That I can trust You and let love happen to the end of my days. Incredible! Amen.

dance

Do one thing every day that scares you. —Eleanor Roosevelt

I can think of lots of warm and fuzzy ways to let love happen. One of my favorite ways to let love happen is to show my kids how precious they are to me. I love to engage. I love to just spend time with them. I love to put that one special something under the Christmas tree and watch them unwrap it. Letting love happen toward my kids gives me the warm fuzzies.

There are other people in my life who are easy to love too. Letting love happen toward my wife is warm fuzzies all around. Letting love happen toward my staff is incredibly rewarding too.

But what about the people in our lives who are difficult to love? What about the people who criticize us and our families? What about the people who don't think the same way we think or live the way we live?

Letting love happen toward them isn't nearly as easy or fun… at least not at first. Frankly, it's a little scary. What if people mistake your love as permission to keep doing what they're doing, or living the way they're living?

Church, we're scared of this, aren't we?

I'm going to tell you a secret: Trust Jesus and let love happen. That's the one thing—the only thing—that matters today.

> *The **only thing** that counts is faith expressing itself through love.*
> (Galatians 5:6, emphasis mine)

How would the gay community feel about the Church if the Church learned to trust Jesus and let love happen toward them?

How many arguments would be diffused if we released the need to defend ourselves and just trusted Jesus and let love happen?

How many believers are locked into cycles of sin because they are afraid to open up and be real? How many people would be set free if we just trusted Jesus and let love happen? If we let go of the need to fix and identify and correct, and we embraced the call to trust Jesus and let love happen?

And how about you? What would your life look like today if you trusted Jesus and let love happen?

Lord, it's hard to let Your love happen after I sin. I want to fix myself and then return to You. It's hard to love others in the midst of their sin. I want to fix them and then present them—and my accomplishment—to You. Forgive me for my arrogance. I want to trust, Lord. I want to trust so I can love today. I can't do this on my own. Create new trust in me, right now, so I can let love happen. Amen.

dance

There's only one catch. Like any other gift, the gift of grace can be yours only if you'll reach out and take it. Maybe being able to reach out and take it is a gift too. —Frederick Buechner

When we step into freedom, there is more opportunity to make poor choices. **So what keeps us—we who are free in Christ—from running toward sin?**

Let's be honest. If we are in Christ, sin can't separate us from God's love anymore. And consequences? Who has received consequences for *every* sin they've ever committed? No one, right? His grace gives us freedom, and His grace even withholds consequences.

So what keeps us from running toward a life of sin?

> *So I say, walk by the Spirit, and you will not gratify the desires of the flesh.* (Galatians 5:16)

Paul is clear. **The trajectory of our life—whether we walk in the Spirit or feed the desires of our flesh—is mapped by a decision.** We can choose the Spirit, or we can choose the flesh.

What, exactly, is the difference between the two?

"Flesh" is not our old sin nature—that has died with Christ. Instead, "flesh" is anything one has—body, mind, emotions, patterns, heritage, education, etc.—that is outside of the divine resources of the Holy Spirit. When we depend on these "fleshly" resources, we are living independently from God. Walking in the Spirit, on the other hand, is living dependently upon God to live through us moment by moment in a dynamic, intimate dance.

If we are walking in the Spirit, we aren't walking in the flesh. The flesh and the Spirit aren't intended to coexist. And so, there's a choice to make. So the question takes us back to your salvation: Were you only saved *from* separation from God? Or were you also saved *to* life in the Spirit?

Giver of Grace, thank you for the gift of choice. This freedom to choose is so full of grace. Show me this dance of dependence as Your Spirit leads. Amen.

dance

You will never cease to be the most amazed person on earth at what God has done for you on the inside. —Oswald Chambers

If the Holy Spirit had been removed from your life last week, would your days have looked different?

Even as believers, we can walk independent of God "in the flesh," rather than depending on the Spirit. And while we might be able to choose between flesh and Spirit, the two aren't complementary—they cannot act harmoniously in the midst of the same circumstance. Truly, this makes our decision tough because the flesh is wired to want things that God doesn't desire for us.

> *For the flesh desires what is contrary to the Spirit, and the Spirit what is contrary to the flesh. They are in conflict with each other, so that you are not to do whatever you want.* (Galatians 5:17)

If you're defining Christian freedom as "getting to do what you want," then you aren't defining it biblically. The more often you reject the desires of the flesh, the less conflict exists within you. So what's the best option? **Consistently walk in the Spirit while learning to recognize the flesh.** Here are some notorious ways the flesh reveals itself:

- **Self-sufficient flesh** convinces you that you can do this on your own. You're strong enough, good-looking enough, and smart enough. You turn to God only when all personal resources are exhausted.

- **Religious flesh** follows all the rules. You struggle with piety and judgment of others. You independently try to be good.

- **Indulgent flesh** seeks numbness or comfort through means other than God. Society calls it an addictive personality as you latch onto things like food, shopping, fantasy novels, substance abuse, or pornography.

- **Sensuous flesh** is drawn toward sensuous things. If it feels good, you do it. You feed your desires and find comfort or numbness—even self-worth and validation—through sex.

All those things might feel like freedom at first. But it's a trap that keeps you from doing what you really want to do in your spirit. The choice is yours today, and what a choice it is: **You can start dancing in the freedom of a Spirit-led life right now, or you can march as a slave to your own flesh.**

Lord, I thank You for your patience. Through Your leading, I can walk in dependence on You. I choose You today. I surrender my self-sufficient, religious, indulgent, sensuous, fleshly desires to You. I ask that You will move through me, leading me moment by moment in a continual walk with Your Spirit today. Amen.

dance

Now we cannot... discover our failure to keep God's law except by trying our very hardest (and then failing)... All this trying leads up to the vital moment at which you turn to God and say, "You must do this. I can't." —C. S. Lewis

Those who have taken the fleshly route know where independence from God leads:

> *The acts of the flesh are obvious: sexual immorality, impurity and debauchery; idolatry and witchcraft; hatred, discord, jealousy, fits of rage, selfish ambition, dissensions, factions and envy; drunkenness, orgies, and the like...* (Galatians 5:19-21)

If we're living life in the flesh, we can expect to experience:

- **Sexual sin**—sexual immorality, impurity, and debauchery
- **Addictions**—idolatry and witchcraft (*Witchcraft* comes from *pharmakeia,* the word we now use for pharmaceuticals.)
- **Relational pain**—hatred, discord, jealousy, rage, selfish ambition, dissensions, factions, and envy
- **Reckless behavior**—drunkenness and orgies and the like...

Part of the Christian life is experiencing profound moral transformation through the indwelling Spirit of God. Still, for some of us it isn't enough to know that God's Spirit is available to work in us, because we are afraid of falling back into the acts of the flesh.

Perhaps you feel like there is something more you should do. If someone would give you a to-do list detailing how to live a good, Christian life, you'd feel so much safer! The Galatian believers shared this desire—this is why they turned to the law, neglected grace, and tried to rid themselves of the acts of the flesh in their own strength. Sure, that seems like the natural thing to do, but it misses the point.

I believe Paul's point to us is this:

- Renounce independence from God.
- Choose to live dependently upon the Spirit.

Author of Acceptance, Lord, I give up. I suffer from perfectionism. All I really wanted was to live this Christian life well. Now I see that even this desire—when lived out of legalism—is rooted in flesh. You must do this. I can't. May Your Spirit usher me into abundant life. I quit trying and ask only that You would live through me moment by moment today, in a vibrant walk in Your Spirit. Amen.

dance

The ego hates losing—even to God. —Richard Rohr

If you were being honest, how much do you trust God's Spirit? Are you the preventative measure person—working ahead of God's Spirit, accomplishing what you can, and asking Him to tie up your loose ends?

Or do you wait on Him to lead and then agree to follow? Are you cool with loose ends and unknowns?

It's hard, isn't it? Relinquishing control goes against the flesh. Our society values independence, and the flesh is all about independence. But God's Kingdom values dependence and unity and surrender.

So where are you in your trust fall with God?

- **Some of you are consistently walking in the Spirit.** None of us are nailing it—that will happen when we meet Jesus—but many are mostly surrendering to the Spirit and living out the benefits! Your relationships show it. You are pure and growing. **It's the best way. So keep going and don't stop.**

- **Some of you are consistently walking in the flesh.** When asked if your life would look any different if the Holy Spirit had been removed, you are like, "Nope. It would be exactly the same." Relationships are full of strife. You gratify impulses. You do what you want rather than how God leads. You're going to destroy relationships and hurt people who love you. It's reckless. **So take the warning! Stop. Trust that the Holy Spirit has your best interests in mind and listen.**

- **A bunch of you do a fantastic job trusting the Holy Spirit in all areas—except those few you like to hold on to, right?** You can't let go of these because, if you were honest, you think you can do a better job with this than He can. You fail to believe in the supreme power of the Holy Spirit. Maybe you control money, relationships, or decisions. **I want to encourage you to let go. Ask the Holy Spirit to take it from you. Tell Him it's His.**

Father, I like to feel safe and in control. Uncertainty scares me and there is a lot of uncertainty in the dance of freedom. Who will I meet? Where will I go? What will it cost? Make surrender and dependence the beat of my heart. I choose to follow You. I choose to trust in You. I rest in the fact that You promise to live out this choice through me. Amen.

Try, try, try just a little bit harder. So I can love, love, love him, I tell myself...
—Janis Joplin

It's always a bummer when you try hard to do something great and it fails.

For example, you do something incredible for your spouse, but it isn't received the way you'd hoped. And you think, *Whatever. See if I do* that *again*.

Or you signed up to serve in kids' ministry and now—while you'd never admit this to anyone—you dread church. All you can think is, *When does my commitment end?*

Or you're parenting these kids that are growing and changing. You're trying to grow with them—give new freedoms and engage in new ways—but you keep feeling rejected. Secretly you wonder, *How long until they move out? This hurts.*

Or maybe you gave money and haven't seen it come back a hundredfold like the guy promised. It's just gone and you feel tricked.

How about this one? You have a friend who's been walking in sin, and you decide it's time to speak the truth in love. Emphasis on truth. Your friend gets up and walks out. You two never talk again.

You tried to do a good work, but it didn't work.

Why don't good works always work? If you sometimes feel more defeated and more exhausted after doing a good work, it's quite possible you are working in the flesh—independently *from* God, even if you're trying hard to please Him.

Good works done in the flesh bring death; but when done in the Spirit, they bring life.

> *For whatever one sows, that will he also reap. For the one who sows to his own flesh will from the flesh reap corruption, but the one who sows to the Spirit will from the Spirit reap eternal life.* (Galatians 6:7-8 ESV)

If you sow in the flesh, you will reap flesh—or death. If you sow in the Spirit, you will reap life.

God, I've been trying to do good works on my own timeline with my own resources and in my own strength. I haven't consulted You before charging ahead, and my life is reaping the results of flesh-works. I'm eager to learn a new way—the way of Your Spirit. So today, I'm giving up on trying in my own strength with my own wisdom. No more trying. Give me the willingness to start depending on You instead. Amen.

DAY 93

dance

A woman had been sleeping next to her dead husband's decomposed corpse for one year until authorities made the grisly discovery this week.
—Cavan Sieczkowski

There are some things in life that just reek—and death is one of them. Most of us hold our breath in the presence of foul odors, or do a 180 and hightail it away.

There's a highway in Texas where skunks go to die. No joke. Shortly after I traded in my truck for a gas-friendly convertible, I was cruising down this highway with the top down. Then I hit Skunk Graveyard. Wow. Gag reflexes and the whole works. It was a nasty smell. If no one picks up the carcass for a couple of days, it's even worse—it's skunk smell and decay.

Good works done in the flesh bring death, decay, and stench—like a two-day-old dead skunk on the side of Highway 544.

> *For the one who sows to his own flesh will from the flesh reap corruption…* (Galatians 6:8 ESV)

But what do we do when the smell of death and decay comes from *us*?!

My wife and I were in a season of marriage when things felt a little off. It was driving me crazy and I just wanted to fix it. So I had this brilliant idea: I went back to the house one afternoon when I knew she would be gone, and I cleaned the house. I did the dishes, vacuumed, and tidied up. I was so excited when I heard the garage door because I knew this good work of mine would make it all better.

I was totally shocked when she looked at the house, then looked at me, and was angry. **Later, she told me she could smell my flesh—my people-pleasing, quick-fixing flesh.**

Some of us do good works in order to evoke specific responses from people. We want them to like us. We need their stamp of approval. So we work in our flesh—independent of God—to manipulate others' opinions of us.

These kinds of good works are not the aroma of Christ, but the aroma of the flesh—the aroma of death, decay, and corruption. They stink like dead skunk on Highway 544. Are you driving your faith down the same road?

Lord, I like to please people just as much as I like to please You, and I'm working myself to death. I feel tired, exhausted, and grumpy. My efforts seem fruitless; if I am honest, they are rotten. Reveal to me my own areas of stink and decay. Replace my flesh with Your Spirit. I want to get off this road, but I can't do it. Please, Lord, steer me away from my flesh into a deeper, more dependent walk with You today. Amen.

I am old, Gandalf. I don't look it, but I am beginning to feel it in my heart of hearts. Well-preserved indeed! Why, I feel all thin, sort of stretched, if you know what I mean: like butter that has been scraped over too much bread. That can't be right. I need a change, or something. —Bilbo Baggins

A daughter loves it when her daddy reminds her of her princess status. With so many voices telling her otherwise, it sounds so good coming from him. She grins. She hugs. She twirls once more.

Sometimes, we need a reminder of our identity in Christ.

- We have died to our old self. We are an entirely new child of God.
- His Spirit lives inside us. His Spirit walks with us and gifts us the wisdom of God.
- Jesus shows Himself through us every day—in relationships and love.

As believers, we don't live by our own strength. We live by the strength of God. **We can rest in Him, dance with Him, find joy in Him because our life is His. And miraculously, His life is ours.**

When we start to feel weary or exhausted, we need a reminder. *Hey, you're trying to live by the flesh again.*

> *But the one who sows to the Spirit will from the Spirit reap eternal life. And let us not grow weary of doing good, for in due season we will reap, if we do not give up.* (Galatians 6:8b-9 ESV)

Weariness comes from working in the flesh. Life comes from the Spirit.

If you're feeling exhausted, ask yourself a few questions:

- Are you serving by your own strength or His?
- Are you serving from love or obligation?
- Are you afraid to let go of something because you don't know what to do if it's gone?

Ask God to remind you of your identity. Ask Him to defeat those desires of your flesh. Dance before your Daddy and feel fully alive once more.

Giver of Eternal Life, I can hardly drag my feet through this life. In the exhaustion of my flesh, life sounds like a prison. I surrender to the Spirit. May the Spirit wage war against my flesh and lead me into a place of freedom. Strengthen my weakness. Nourish my soul. Then pour me out before others so they can be free too. Amen.

If opportunity doesn't knock, build a door. —Milton Berle

An unexpected bonus of raising teens is getting to know their friends. One particular friend seemed to be having a hard time. The slump in this kid's shoulders told us something was up. As we prayed for this teen, I felt compelled to sit down and share with him the story of my own teenage years. *No problem, God. I can do that.*

So I waited for the perfect opportunity to talk, but none came. A week passed and I hadn't said anything. The Spirit was really pressing in and I was really trying to listen.

Finally, God gave me a brilliant idea. I put a plate of cookies on the table. Cookies are teen magnets. Sure enough, this kid was sitting across the table from me within five minutes. I shared some thoughts and when I finished, this quiet kid opened up and shared that he felt invisible.

I believe the Holy Spirit wanted this kid to know that the Lord is *El Roi*—the God Who Sees him.

Following the Spirit can be as simple as a plate of cookies and a dining room table. It can be as simple as a story. There are opportunities all around us to walk in the Spirit and serve in love.

How can you know what good works the Spirit would have you do?

> *Therefore, as we have opportunity, let us do good to all people, especially to those who belong to the family of believers.* (Galatians 6:10)

As opportunities present themselves, serve all people. Is it going to cost something? Yes, you might have to get creative and whip up some cookies. You might have to knock on a neighbor's door and ask if they need help. You might need to chat it up in the checkout line and get to know someone. But the effort is worth it, isn't it? To know that—in your everyday routine—you are walking with the Spirit and serving in love.

When presented with an opportunity to serve, surrender it to the Spirit and let Him love through you. That's pretty simple.

God Who Sees, I can't see the hearts of all like You can. I can't know their fears or circumstances or stories like You know them. But through Your Spirit, I can love with Your love. Open my eyes to the opportunities to engage. Give me the stamina to serve all. Amen.

dance

I want a 100% kind of relationship, and I'm willing to give it 50%.
—Jarod Kintz

There are some places you shouldn't stop halfway—a road, for instance. Maybe you're thinking, *Well, Pete, I'm a middle-of-the-road kind of person.*

To which I'd answer, "Middle-of-the-road people get hit by cars."

Listen, there really are some things in life that require you to go 100 percent of the distance or you'll miss out on life, and maybe even get killed.

I was in Hong Kong in 1982, shortly after the Chinese border reopened to Westerners. My friend had grown up as a missionary kid in China, so he offered to take me into China. When we arrived at the border, there was a bridge. On that bridge we were neither in Hong Kong nor China. What if we'd said, "You know what? We're tired. Why don't we stop here in this no man's land?"

Immediately following our wedding reception, Libby and I went and grabbed a bite to eat. It was a magical moment. We were no longer single, but we weren't *totally* married. And so we just sat there, staring at each other. I'd have been foolish if I'd said, "This moment is so special. Let's just stay here forever."

What would you say to someone who wants to know God through Scripture but stopped reading at the end of Malachi, where God says, "*Or else I will come and strike the land with total destruction*" (Malachi 4.6b)?

You might shout, "Don't stop with the Old Testament! Flip the page! The best stuff is next!"

Here's the deal: Many of you are stuck in between legalism and grace. You've realized no performance can please God, so you've stopped. You're jumping around, shouting, "I don't have to! I don't have to!"

But you haven't yet stepped into, "I get to! I get to!"

You've realized the emptiness of marching, and you've decided to stop. This is such a great start. But don't stop before you become a dancer. Don't stand in the middle of the road between law and grace. **Living life half-surrendered to God's Spirit isn't the adventure God has for you.**

Lord, I've stopped marching and I am so excited! But I know there is more to the Christian life than simply leaving the law behind. Prepare me to go the full distance. Transform me so that I'm "all in." Lead me into the dance. Amen.

When you arise in the morning, think of what a precious privilege it is to be alive—to breathe, to think, to enjoy, to love. —Marcus Aurelius

You got the message: **God loves me and I don't have to do X anymore.**

You left Old Covenant living behind. You abandoned legalism. You stopped marching because New Covenant living looks a lot different—more like a dance.

But you aren't dancing yet. Instead, you're stuck between "I don't have to!" and "I get to!" And it feels a little like wilderness, like the Israelites felt after they left the bondage of Egypt. They had seen "gods" humbled, death reign, seas parted, and rocks gush water. Yet, as they stood at the edge of the Promised Land and took a vote on whether or not they should enter, the Israelites lamented their lost days of slavery! They *wished* for bondage.

> *And they said to each other, "We should choose a leader and go back to Egypt."* (Numbers 14:4)

In His grace, God allowed them to refuse entrance to all He had promised. Instead, He had them wander the wilderness between bondage and blessing.

Wilderness wandering is exactly what the Israelites did until death. That generation missed the adventure.

I'm so grateful you've stopped marching. I don't want you in Egypt— under the bondage of the law. But neither do I want you wandering in the wilderness.

So, yes, God loves you and you don't **have** to do X anymore. But what do you **get** to do with Him?

To whom do you **get** to give generously?

Whom do you **get** to serve?

What conversation do you **get** to have with Him today?

Holy Spirit, I realize the magnificent role You fill in my everyday life with Christ. Lead this dance. I get to follow You—what an adventure! Open my eyes to the things we get to do together today, then do those things through me in Your joy and strength. Amen.

dance

The good news is that Christ frees us from the need to obnoxiously focus on our goodness, our commitment, and our correctness… Jesus invited us to a dance… —Steve Brown

There's white space in Paul's letter to the Galatians, where we can get stuck.

> *Not even those who are circumcised keep the law, yet they want you to be circumcised that they may boast about your circumcision in the **flesh. May** I never boast except in the cross of our Lord Jesus Christ, through which the world has been crucified to me, and I to the world.* (Galatians 6:13-14, emphasis mine)

Look at the little section in bold in that verse. Look right after the period and before the M. **See that speck of white on the page? That's our white space.** Before this white space, Paul speaks of marching. After, Paul speaks of dancing.

So the question is: Are you living pre-, post-, or mid-white space?

- Marchers boast of their own strength and external appearances.
- Dancers boast in the strength of the cross.

It's that simple. Are you trying hard to make yourself a better Christian? Do you tally your quiet times? Do you volunteer but complain? Do you reluctantly write checks? This is marching, friends. This is pre-white space.

Or…

Are you resting in Christ, allowing Him to shape you as He wishes? Are you soaking up intimate time with Jesus, wishing for more? Do you find yourself drawn toward hurting people? Do you find great joy in giving generously as the Spirit leads? Do you naturally share the reality of Christ within you through your actions and words? Have you released comfortable life in exchange for God's adventure? These are some ways of dancing, friends.

And then there is the white space.

In the white space a transformed person affects *nothing*. The white-space dweller lives a self-consumed faith. No one is served. No love is shared. No stories of the cross are told.

If you're living in the white space, it's just you and Jesus. You aren't marching, but you aren't dancing… yet.

Jesus, I'm free, but in many ways I'm stuck in the white space. I hear Your invitation. Give me the courage to boast in Your dance, even if I stumble in the steps at first. Show me today, Lord, just one more step to take in Your Spirit. Just one more step at a time. Amen.

dance

If we get our information from the biblical material, there is no doubt that the Christian life is a dancing, leaping, daring life. —Eugene Peterson

Living in the white space—between releasing legalism and living by the Spirit—is dangerous, friends. The restraining nature of the law is gone, but you're not yet functioning in the power of the Spirit. It's easy to indulge in whatever pleases you.

Take a look at these two huge areas and see how they differ from each other, depending on whether you're marching, dancing, or stuck in between:

Marching & Serving
You used to be serving, but you only did it because the Sunday announcements left you feeling guilty. No more! Performance-based serving is over.

Dancing & Serving
You prayerfully ask God for opportunities to use your gifts and talents. You know He's prepared these ahead of you, so you keep your eyes peeled to serve.

White Space & Self-Serving
It feels so good to be void of obligation! What to do with all this free time? You decide to pursue hobbies and interests. Pretty soon, your calendar is booked with things to do, and there doesn't seem to be time for anyone else.

Marching & Giving
You were taught God demands 10 percent—whether you're filing for bankruptcy or clearing all of your bills with a surplus. Not anymore. You are free from the tithe. You realize you can stop, so you do.

Dancing & Giving
Envisioning freedom, you decide to pay off debt and dream of the day when you have more to give. Or maybe you realize your budget has more than a tenth available to invest in God's Kingdom, so you sit down with your kids and brainstorm generosity.

White Space & Self-Giving
You are so excited to be able to do whatever you want with your money. But you quickly get sucked into materialism. What you once shared, you now invest in yourself. It's a different kind of slavery.

This white space can swallow us up in self-indulgence. But dancing is focused on the leading of the Spirit. It's where the adventure is found!

Lord, I don't want self-love to consume what could be Spirit-led. Self-love leaves me wanting. Instead, I open my hands to You—fill them with Yours and lead me in the dance of sacrifice, selflessness, and service. Amen.

dance

Legalism wrenches the joy of the Lord from the Christian believer…
—S. Lewis Johnson

Dancing would be a whole lot easier if someone would just show us all how to exactly move our bodies. Then we'd all be dancing the same dance; and if I felt like I was messing up, I could look over and compare my dance steps to yours. And if I felt like you were messing up, then I could tell you.

Wait a minute. That sounds a lot like marching—like living by the law.

Let me tell you what happens when you, your family, and your church family all start dancing: **Your walk with Jesus starts looking different than theirs. The Holy Spirit knows each of us intimately and leads us according to our gifts, our design, and even our weaknesses.**

But there are general characteristics that all dancers will display.

> *May I never boast except in the cross of our Lord Jesus Christ, through which the world has been crucified to me, and I to the world. Neither circumcision nor uncircumcision means anything; what counts is the new creation.* (Galatians 6:14-15)

- Dancers boast in the cross.
- Dancers die to the world and its influence.
- Dancers embrace the new creation.

The contrast is not always obvious, but it's profound:

- Marchers boast in their own accomplishments, but dancers know life begins at the cross.

- Marchers battle sin on their own, but dancers die to the world and let the Spirit live through them.

- Marchers use the law as a checklist for living, but dancers embrace the new creation that is the Christian life—new nature, new desires, and new habits.

- The marcher's melody is law, but the dancer's movements are grace-filled.

So if you're afraid of looking different in the dance, then I want to reassure you—you'll look totally different. We each need grace for different things in our lives. Sure, we are dancing in the same Spirit, but our dances are individually choreographed. He will lead you differently.

Lord of the Dance, as I dance with You, I realize that You lead intimately—knowing my personality, struggles, desires, and talents. Fill my line of vision so I stop copying the steps of others and let You lead me into the adventurous, abundant life in the Spirit. Amen.

More from Pete and *Telling the Truth*

Devotionals like these are available by subscribing to Pete's daily email devotional, *Experiencing Life Today*, at **tellingthetruth.org**. You can also access a library of Bible-teaching resources from Pete and his parents, Stuart and Jill Briscoe, including audio and video sermons, articles, books, study materials, and other tools to help you grow in your knowledge of God's Word and experience Life in Christ in all its fullness.

You can also hear Pete on *Telling the Truth*'s daily 30-minute Bible-teaching program, broadcast on over 500 radio stations across the United States, United Kingdom, and beyond. Find a station near you or listen online at **tellingthetruth.org**, or download the free *Telling the Truth* app from your mobile store.